THE DAN DUNN-HARCOURT FEUD

Steve Harcourt's first shot ricocheted and drilled the picture of John L. Sullivan. Dunn shot Steve twice and killed him.

Carl Guldberg

INCREDIBLE SENEY

By

Lewis C. Reimann

INCREDIBLE SENEY

by

Lewis C. Reimann

Copyright 1982
by
Avery Color Studios
AuTrain, Michigan 49806

Library of Congress No. 81-71825
ISBN 0-932212-26-3
First Edition - 1982
Reprinted - April, 1984

INCREDIBLE SENEY was originally published in 1953 with copyright secured by Lewis C. Reimann.

Other books by the Author
Between the Iron and the Pine
When Pine Was King

"LET NO ONE SAY, AND
SAY IT TO MY SHAME,
THAT ALL WAS BEAUTY,
UNTIL I CAME"

Legend at the Hartwick Pines,
the Last Stand of Michigan's Virgin Pine,
Grayling, Michigan

Acknowledgments

This third book dealing with the pioneer life in the Upper Peninsula of Michigan has been written with the assistance of many witnesses of the early scenes of that rugged period—old time lumberjacks, woods bosses, descendants of the pioneer families and many others interested in those hardy people.

Among those who contributed to the volume were John I. Bellaire of Manistique, whose voluminous records and vivid recollections were invaluable; John J. Riordan of Seney, who came upon the scene in the waning lumbering days; Jack Mitchell, lumbercamp foreman and riverman; Joe Curry, engineer on the logging railroads for fifty years; George H. Hedquist, lumber broker of Detroit, whose continued interest in the author's attempt to bring back those tales of the time "when men were men" is deeply appreciated; and many others.

The Leech papers in the Michigan historical Collections at the University of Michigan, Michigan Writers Project of the depression days, several newspapers and magazines on early Michigan lumbering have each furnished material of value.

Photographs were generously furnished by the Burton Historical Collection of Detroit, George H. Hedquist, John J. Riordan and others. Line drawings by Carl E. Gulberg.

Dr. F. Clever Bald of the Michigan Historical Collections at the University of Michigan was most helpful in making records available.

To the above people and institutions the author acknowledges his indebtedness in making this factual volume possible.

CHAPTER ONE

Incredible Seney

SENEY, the lumber town half way between Sault Ste. Marie and Wakefield, during the Eighties and Nineties was said to have been the toughest town in Michigan's Upper Peninsula. It had the reputation of having out-cut, out-logged, out-fought, out-drank and out-sported the rest of the world in its heyday.

During the last great stand of white pine left in Michigan's war on its virgin timber, Seney was no virgin, and should anyone at that time have ascribed that virtue to her, hundreds of lumberjacks, saloon keepers and gamblers, as well as its law abiding citizens would have risen to dispute it.

A rough, lawless town of 3000 people even in its quieter moments, it became a place of riot, drinking and "loving" when the horde of 3000 more descended upon it at the spring breakup of the fifteen or more lumber camps in the surrounding woods. The twenty-one saloons, the four or five blind pigs, the three brothels in the town and the two brothels up the river threw away the keys to their front doors as the men came in, wild for whiskey, the fighting and the women and ran day and night, law or no law and to hell with the sheriff.

Drifting tales of license and corruption brought Seney an investigating committee of newspaper reporters, seek-

1

ing lurid tales which they might spread in bold headlines in their papers. Among them was a woman reporter, one of the few of the day. Unimpressed by the open gambling, fighting, drinking and prostitution, she began her report with the story of the "Ram Pasture."

Indeed, she wired her newspaper, the rumors from wild and wide-open Seney were true—and more, the place was a hell-camp of slavery. Strangers were being shanghaied on the frontier, shunted into box cars to the camps, held in chained peonage, tracked down by fierce dogs when they attempted to escape. Forced to work in the dark forest by day, they were herded into camp at nightfall and held in the "Ram Pasture," a great log stockade unfit for dumb animals. The place was so overcrowded that the chained men were forced to sleep in shifts.

This story made the headlines in all the metropolitan dailies. The writer became a successful and sensational sober-sister overnight. A congressional committee was kept out of the district only through the efforts of a Wall Street lumber baron and Michigan politicians, who denied the whole story indignantly, stating that a hoax had been played upon the newspaper woman by obliging practical jokers who wanted her to find what she was looking for, a lurid, sensational tale. They declared that the "fierce dogs" were mastiffs raised by a local saloon keeper for sale; that the Ram Pasture was the main floor of a crowded hotel where the management permitted men to sleep in eight hour shifts when the lumber camps broke up in the spring and the rooming houses were over-crowded, on payment of the regular rates in advance, and that the armed guards merely insured the prompt removal of the sleeping men when their time was up.

There was no slavery, for who could enslave a wild lumberjack? There was no shanghaiing, for no jack could ever be controlled. There was no stockade which an able-bodied woodsman could not bust through. In fact the abuse of freedom was the cause of the trouble any lumber jack was guilty of. Inquiring officials of the government were mollified by this report but the general public, having heard the wild tales, was never quite convinced. The first story had been so sensational, so vividly portrayed and so often repeated in the newspapers, magazines and around home firesides that there are people today who still believe the old tales. Even present day tourists drive their cars miles off their intended route to see the wild Seney lumberjacks fighting on the streets, the wide open saloons and the red-curtained houses of infamy.

Today the inquisitive visitor to Seney will find a ghost community of its former self with only 250 residents, four gas stations, one lonely bar and two general stores. A small factory there builds prefabricated homes out of the slimly gleaned trees from the cut-over, burned-over land that once was an almost impenetrable pine forest. Several modern homes with bathrooms, oil and gas heat, running water and electricity have been built to give the lie to stories of earlier days. A four room brick veneer school houses the children of today with no fear of marauding lumberjacks who once chewed up the plank sidewalks with their calked boots and each other's ears with their tobacco stained teeth in that earlier era. The only wild life one sees now in the vicinity of Seney are the numberless deer, an occasional bear, thousands of wild fowl in

3

the vast swamp preserves and the wild hunters who come from the cities of Lower Michigan, with cars loaded with cases of whiskey and in a number of instances with equally wild women brought along for the occasion.

CHAPTER TWO

A Reputation Not Unearned

W HETHER OR NOT there was slavery, the lawless reputation of early Seney was not unearned. Should you question Jack Mitchell, a former lumber camp foreman and river driver who lives in his white painted pine house amid the jackpines at the edge of town today, he will quickly tell you from personal experience what a hellhole Seney was in his youth and young manhood. He will tell you of the scores of fancy women who came in on the morning train from Marquette in the spring, plied their trade openly even in livery stables because the other "hoodlums" were already overcrowded, stuff their bosoms with greenbacks either given by the lumberjacks or stolen from them in their drunken stupor, then returned to Marquette on the evening train to continue the sale of their bodies in that northern city.

Few places of its size ever had quite so many picturesque characters as this mad community. As the lumber camps in southern Michigan cleaned off the virgin pine and moved across the Straits of Mackinaw, characters of all description moved with them to the cuttings in the famous Seney Swamp—bona fide lumberjacks seeking work at the only employment they knew, saloon keepers seeking the easy money which the jacks spent recklessly, gamblers, procurers, loose women, refugees from the law and a few business men.

The most notorious figure of the horde who came north was a railroad section hand, Leon Czolgosz, who later assassinated President McKinley. Another was P. K. Small, better known as "Snag Jaw," who regularly earned his drinks by biting off the heads of live snakes and frogs. His end came one day when he extended his talent by biting off the head of a pet crow in a brothel. For this P. K. was laid low with a heavy peavey handle.

"Stuttering" Jim Gallagher left his mark—mostly with his hobnail driving shoes on the faces of those who found his speech amusing. "Protestant" Bob McQuire was a peaceful man with thumbnails like bowie knives. He seldom fought but when he did his opponent emerged from the combat with gaping wounds across his face and throat.

"Stub Foot" O'Donnell and "Pump Handle" Joe met incoming trains, stood strangers on their heads and shook loose change from their pockets for liquor money. "Old Light Heart," who liked raw liver, which he could get free at the butcher shop, and slept in two sugar barrels turned end to end, eventually lost his toes by frost bite. Whenever he got drunk after that "Pump Handle" Joe and his crony, "Frying Pan Mag," amused themselves by nailing "Old Light Heart's" shoes to the floor.

The slickest gambler about the place was "Wiry" Jim Summers, who wore two guns in sight but carried a derringer in his clothes for "self-protection," using it after his enemy had apparently disarmed him: "Fighting Jim" Morrison was the undisputed king of the plank sidewalks and those who failed to give way when they met him just "weren't real bright."

But the mightiest of the mighty was "Silver Jack" Driscoll whose trail of fighting led him all the way from the woods of Canada, to Maine, to Seney and to an unmarked grave in L'Anse on the shores of Keewenaw Bay. After spending a term in Michigan State Prison at Jackson for strongarming a lumberjack of $2.50, he served as a bartender and bouncer for the notorious Dan Dunn at Seney.

Innumerable are the tales of the he-men who swaggered their way into Seney, cut the pine, fought the battle of the bottle and at last succumbed to their invincible enemy, John Barleycorn.

Seney in the early days was a much abused town. "Once tough, always tough" seemed to have been her fate. It became the gathering place of some of the toughest elements in the north. How she got her name is still a matter of dispute but of her reputation there is no doubt. By some it is claimed that she was named for a railroad contractor who built the Duluth, South Shore and Atlantic Railroad. Others insist that her name came about through the mispronunciation of an appellation which early lumberjacks found hard to mouth. This story has it that a certain Jewish fur buyer had set up a fur trading post, called the "Sheeny's Place." Gradually it b e c a m e "Sheeny," then Seney. However it came about, the town became the byword for toughness and lawlessness wherever lumbermen gathered.

About the first arrivals in Seney were a crew of woodsmen from the Saginaw Valley lumber camps, known as the Valley Boys, who on their way upkicked the windows out of the passenger coaches of their train, fortelling the life which was to be. They pitched Carlson, the proprietor

7

of the big boarding house, who served their first supper, into a snow bank because the steak was tough.

The climate and the terrain of the area was just as rugged as the Valley Boys that first winter. The snow was six feet deep on the level. The thick ice blocked the water in the Fox River until the entire swamp land was covered. Bodies of drowned and frozen deer frequently floated on the crest of the stream. Plank sidewalks were built on cedar posts two and three feet above the ground, with water all around, making it a hazardous staging for the bibulous jacks as they careened from saloon to saloon.

Seney characters were "storybook people," products of an unbelieveable time when individualism was permitted to reach extremes. No modern fiction could paint them as they were without being charged with exaggeration. In addition to the characters mentioned, there was "Roaring Jim" Gleason, "Black Jack" McDonald, "Handsome Jack" O'Toole, "Runaway" Shea, "Buck Pete," "Blue Jay," "Pigfoot" and scores of others, who helped make history in the pine woods and riot in the town. "Jackson Heinz" still lives today in Stewart Edward White's "The Blazed Trail."

Today a ten cent lock hangs from the door of Seney's empty jail which temporarily housed such inebriates who were too far gone to resist the frightened town marshall in the 80's. Cows graze near the spot where Hughie Logan and "Runaway" Shea engaged in their epic rough and tumble fight. A gasoline pump looms red where "Tim" Kaine, the giant lumbercamp boss, was stabbed by Isaac Stecher on a Christmas Eve while Santa Claus was distributing sacks of candy and popcorn to the children of the town.

JOHNNY HUNT AND WIFE
Johnny, a conductor on the Manistique R.R., had his train windows
kicked out by lumberjacks.

The dramatic stage where these characters played their part is gone, burned down or removed elsewhere, but ask any oldtimer and he will tell you of those hearties who, twirling their fierce mustaches and stomping their steel-shod boots, came along with the most astounding collection of outcasts, gamblers, rouges and scamps that Michigan and Schoolcraft county ever knew.

CHAPTER THREE

The Early Scene At Seney

It is from the vivid recollection and the facile pen of John I. Bellaire that most of the colorful tales of early Seney come. Now a man of eighty years, John lives a quiet life in Manistique. Talk to any oldtimer who claims "I was there when it happened" and he will tell you that Bellaire tales are gross exaggeration, that John was not on the scene "when it happened." In fact no two alleged witnesses of an incident at Seney will give the same account. If all the men who swear they were present in Dan Dunn's saloon at the time the latter shot Steve Harcourt, the place must have held one hundred and fifty people. Nevertheless, Bellaire's account of his several years residence in Seney contains the basic facts.

Fresh from a few years of teaching in a small country school in Lower Michigan, Bellaire came to Seney to clerk in the general store operated by Morse and Schneider, which catered to lumber camps, lumberjacks, town families and the people of the whole area. John had seen lumberjacks in his home town but was hardly prepared for the scenes which opened up in his new location. Getting off the D.S.S.&A.R.R. station at noon he headed for the store. When Morse asked him if he did not want to spend his first afternoon looking about him in the village, he replied:—

11

"No, I've seen enough coming from the depot."

His first assignment was to deliver groceries to the American House, owned and operated by "Daddy" O'-Brien and his pugnatious wife.

"With a bushel of potatoes and several small packages," relates Bellaire, "I passed Hugh Logan's saloon. A lumberjack, Walter Bens, stepped behind me, grabbed my hat and tossed it into the saloon behind the bar, ordering me to either treat, drink or take a thrashing. I told him I would do neither and went bareheaded to the hotel to make my delivery.

"At the hotel I entered the large kitchen where Mrs. O'Brien was peeling the few potatoes she had on hand. The woman met me at the door with the knife in her hand and a scowl on her face, yelling:

' "This is a foine toime to deliver them groceries! How in hell do you expect me to get supper ready in toime for all our hungry boarders at this late hour?" '

"I saw there was no use trying to explain that Bens had stolen my hat, so I set the basket down and bounded out of the door and back to the store. As I passed the saloon Bens was there waiting for me and demanded to know what I intended to do about accepting his kind invitation. As Bens reached for my coat collar, Billy Marks, the bartender, came out and laughingly tossed me my hat, advising me to pay no attention to Bens, for that was his way of getting a free drink. Bens explained that he merely intended to initiate me.

"Had I entered the saloon the lumberjacks would have hoisted me to the top of the bar and ordered me to stand treat. Had I done that, they would not have harmed me and the fun would have been over.

Howard Bros.,   Manistigue, Mich.

"EDUCATED" MEN OF SENEY, 1895
John I. Bellaire, standing left, was postmaster, store clerk and local
historian.

"That afternoon Mrs. O'Brien came to the store and with a twinkle in her Irish eyes asked me why I had run when she started to meet me with the groceries. I answered:

" 'Why, lady, when I saw that mad expression on your face and the butcher knife in your hand, I took no chances.' "

Bellaire recounts endless tales of his days in his new position. The seasonal nature of the lumbering operations was the reason for ebb and flow of the erratic life in Seney. It was said that there were three crews of lumberjacks—one crew working in the woods, one spending its time in town and one returning to work in the woods.

Seney had many derelict lumberjacks, men beyond the point where they could hold or want a regular job in the camps. These were given the job of "road monkey," a menial work of cutting out skidding roads in the deep woods or as chore boys in the camp. Their pay was small and they had little left in their account at the end of the cutting season, having spent most of their money for tobacco, clothes and occasional bootleg liquor.

When these old jacks returned to town, they would do almost anything for a drink after their little poke was spent. They mooched their drinks from the more prosperous woodsmen, "ran their faces" for liquor at the bar or swept the sawdust covered floor and cleaned the "goboons" early in the morning before the taverns opened. On warm mornings before opening time dozens of lumberjacks would be seen sitting on the edge of the plank sidewalks watching for the first sign of smoke rolling out of the tavern chimneys indicating that the bartender had arrived. Upon the appearance of life in the establish-

ments each moocher would silently hotfoot it to his favorite place where he might be successful in getting a free
"eye-opener." "Skid-row" was well established there and
its members were ever present on the street, waiting,
staggering or mooching. They were the original men from
the "skidding road" of the woods to become the men of
"skid row" of today.

When time hung heavily on their hands, some of the
men resorted to practical jokes which might bring them
treats from the onlookers. Commercial travelers at times
met indignity and financial disaster when they mixed
with the drinking floaters. Looked upon as "city dudes"
and "greenhorns" from "Down Below," as Lower Michigan was called, they were always legitimate and easy
prey for the pranksters.

Dave Beatty, a salesman for the Lee and Cady Grocery
Company of Detroit, came to town at frequent intervals.
He was known as "a swell dresser" and a handsome dude.
After his business was over and his orders were in the
mail, he often "hit the high spots" of Seney.

One morning after a particularly gay night, Beatty
came down to the barroom in the Grondin Hotel for a few
shots of "the hair of the dog that bit him." About twenty
of the woods boys were assembled there. Beatty flashed
a five dollar bill onto the bar and told the barkeep to give
the boys a round of drinks. The invitation was quickly
accepted. This meant that he was expected to drink with
each of the lumberjacks in turn, for as long as a man
had money in his pocket the ethics demanded that he
treat in turn. Before the salesman could accommodate
them all he was ready to go "under the table." He staggered to a large chair and was soon fast asleep.

15

Two of the lumberjacks looked him over, at his city clothes, his new hat and his high button shoes with their "bulldog" toes.

"How would you look dressed up like that, Mike?" asked one.

"Well, there is only one way to find out," replied his pal.

Together they picked up the limp salesman and carried him to his upstairs room where they removed all his clothes and dressed Mike up in his apparel, even to his shirt, shoes and necktie. Then they dressed Beatty in Mike's rough lumberwoods clothes, boots and all. Taking the money the sleeping man had in his pockets, his railroad ticket, watch and personal belongings, they placed them in the pockets of the clothes they had dressed him in. His flashy tie pin they fastened on the mackinaw where he would find it. Then the pair sauntered out to parade Mike in all the saloons of the town.

Beatty did not awaken until the next morning. Stiff and sore and with a balloon-like head, he rubbed his aching joints. He felt of his rough clothes and came upright with a jerk. He looked into the cloudy mirror over the dresser to see a disheveled lumberjack staring back at him. He dug into his pockets and found his possessions intact.

Holding onto the handrail he rushed downstairs to the proprietor and demanded an explanation. The owner, innocent of what had happened, made a search but found no clue to the jokers.

Beatty sat down to consider his plight. He could not appear on the street in his newly acquired outfit. Then he staggered up to his room, packed his grip and sample case and took the next train for the Soo, where he used part of his expense money to buy a new suit, shoes, shirt and necktie. A few days later the jokers appeared on the street again, Mike wearing the fancy button shoes and a white shirt under lumberjack clothes.

George Raymond was a secretive person. Where he came from and what his life had been, no one knew. He gave no hint. His hands were small and his speech refined—a sharp contrast to the rough men with whom he associated in the camps. It was rumored that he had been a public official from down below and had absconded with public funds. What his real name was no one ventured to ask him. In his cups he recited the Illiad and the Oddessy in Greek. Sober, he was reserved and unsocial. As in many cases where unknowns drifted into the north woods country, no questions were asked and no explanations given. A man's worth there was measured by his skill with an ax and his capacity for hard liquor.

Foreign labor was imported by the lumber and railroad companies—men from Poland, Russia, the Scandanavian countries, Germany, Italy and Austria—to get out the pine and work on the railroads which hauled it out. Foreign names were puzzling to Bill McPherson, the general lumber company clerk, so he simplified them in his records. Michael Zbronszkivich he named Mike Broncho. Anthony Krzyminski became Tony Mink. He explained to them that these simplified names would be their lumber camp or American names, some of which still cling to the members of their families who live today.

Swan Swanson had come over from Sweden to seek his fortune in the north country. An efficient woodsman and a clever axeman, he was paid the highest prevailing wage. As he worked he saved his money. His mastery of English did not keep up with his increasing bank account. After several years of saving and scrimping, he sailed back to Sweden to visit his family and friends. There he persuaded his nephew of the same name to come to America with him. On the return boat trip in steerage, Swan carefully coached his nephew, Swan Swanson, in his limited English.

"Skal det man at da dock esk you vat you name is you skal say after me: ' "sam tang, yust like my onkle!"

When the immigration officer asked the elder Swan, the American lumberjack, what his name was, the latter replied:—

"Swan Swanson, by yimminy."

"And what is your name, young man?" he asked the nephew, who replied:—

"Sam tang, by yimminy, yust like my onkle."

And Sam Tang he is called to this day, this name appearing thus in the directory of one of the U.P. towns.

The influence of Emma Goldman, the notorious anarchist, was felt even in the remote area around Seney, although there was no labor movement there at the time and workmen in the woods and the railroad accepted the going wages of a dollar a day and "found." Occasionally an "agitator" appeared in the lumber towns but was given "short shift" by both the camp operators and the workmen. Content with their meagre wages and the life they lived, few gave ear to the malcontents.

However, one individual affected by the new movement which was infesting the peace of the world was a short time resident of Seney. Leon Czolgolz worked as a section hand on the Manistique Railroad, swinging a pick

Early Seney residents dressed up. John Chisolm, lower left, was Supt. of the Alger-Smith Lumber Company.

and a tamping shovel under Tony Mink, who had become the section boss. Czolgolz was born in Detroit of Russian parents and in his youth had come under the spell of Emma Goldman. When his activities in Detroit became too hot he drifted north and finally landed a job on the railroad. Here he was a continuous source of trouble to his boss, an agitator for workmen's rights and a violent advocate of anarchism.

Discharged for his trouble making on the section, Czolgolz was dismissed amid the jeers of his fellow workers. A few years later, on September 6th, 1901, he shot President William McKinley at Buffalo, declaring him to be "the enemy of the good working people."

CHAPTER FOUR

Some Good In Seney

S ENEY had its good side, rough as it was in its day. The hearts of even the roughest could be touched when the need for assistance arose in the community. The rank and file of the lumberjacks were not an entirely bad lot. Their pay was small, but few of them ever refused to give of their little when a fellow workman met misfortune.

Work in the woods was hazardous. Sharp axes frequently bit deep into human flesh and bone. Trees did not always fall in the exact direction intended and men were caught under their crashing impact. Snow-covered logs had a way of rolling over a man's leg. Log jams on the spring drive took their toll of human lives.

Lumber companies assumed little or no responsibility for accidents or illness. Once a lumberjack became sick or disabled while working in the camp he was shipped out on the next supply sleigh to the nearest town, there to recover as best he might or died from his disability. Horses in the camps were more valuable and received better care than the shifting crew. If the native labor supply was short, labor agents in Europe could always ship a boatload of immigrant greenhorns across the Atlantic and by cattle cars to the lumber camps, docile hands who did no complaining or agitating and did not know the difference between a cant hook and a cross-haul.

John O'Day, a married man with a wife and three small children, was a typical lumberjack. After the spring breakup O'Day struck out for Seney where his family lived, but that stop at the first saloon overcame his love of family. Most of his winter's stake was spent with the boys and there was little left when he reached his shack late that night. The family was destitute. O'Day's money was gone. His credit at the general store was at an end. His smallest daughter was lying on a crude cot, ill with dyptheria. O'Day stayed home for a few days, then with a sense of guilt asked a neighbor woman to come in to take care of his family while he went off to the spring drive to earn the high wages offered to the "river hogs."

Sandy Morrison, a Scotchman and a leader among the rivermen, heard about the destitute family and set out from the Fox River where he was working to investigate. He found little food in the house. The neighbor woman had failed to appear. The child had grown worse. Going to the Morse and Schneider general store he asked the assistance of John Bellaire, to draw up a petition to help the family and put down his name for one dollar to be taken out of his pay. Bellaire signed to give a dollar, too.

Sandy then returned to the river drive and as he met the men along the way he asked them to sign and donate to the needy family. The next day he and O'Day returned to Seney with $158.00, a huge amount in those days. Once in the little house O'Day burst into tears at the plight he had brought on his brood. Sandy called Dr. E. P. Bohn to administer to them and hired a woman to care for them. Next he went to the store and requested

Bellaire to send them a month's supply of food, remarking:

"This will mean a few less drinks for us when the drive is over but it will do this man's family a world of good. Tomorrow I'm taking O'Day back with me up the river. He'll have a good month's wages coming when we get the logs to the mill and I'll see that the check is made out to his wife this time."

In a camp north of Seney one of the cutters misjudged the direction in which a tree would fall and was pinned under its top. A broken limb drove through his body from front to back. He was carried to the camp bunkhouse and a messenger was dispatched to Seney for Dr. Bohn. The man was writhing in desperate pain when the doctor arrived. The medical man found the ends of the limb protruding from the man's body. He secured a handsaw from the tool shed and cut the limb off at each end, loaded the unfortunate man into a horse-drawn sleigh, covered him with rough camp blankts and set off through the snow-covered road for Seney. There he carefully anesthetized him and drew out the broken limb. The operation was successful and the man lived to fell trees again.

When the men came into the camp that evening and heard about the accident, they trooped into the camp office and each said to the camp clerk:—

"Charge a dollar to my account."

Within half an hour $87.00 was raised for their injured companion. Their hearts were as big as their frames were rugged.

Dr. Bohn, fresh out of medical school, served the men in the woods, their families and the people of Seney and the surrounding territory for many years until the pine gave out and the town went down to the extent that one could buy abandoned homes there for the price of their doors and window frames. Dr. Bohn needed no medical association to guide him in the ethics of his practise. He was there to serve whomever and wherever his skill was needed. His fees were ridiculously small. A call into the deep woods through blinding blizzards and below zero weather would often bring him just a few dollars in return. Many times there was no possibility to collect. These accounts were simply charged to "service" and were never entered in his books, if he kept books, which was doubtful.

The hearts of these rough men were not as hard as their work. No matter how indifferent or case-hardened the outer man might have appeared, there usually lived inside that rugged interior a deep feeling which could be aroused by a friends' affliction, the magic presence of a good woman or the touch of a child's hand.

At times a quarter of venison, a side of beef or a mess of brook trout were often brought in payment for the doctor's services. Some bills of years standing were paid when the patient came on better days. Dr. Bohn's Hippocratic Oath, which he took when he completed his two years in medical school, was his sole guide in serving his people in that isolated and rugged area about Seney.

However, the isolation of the camps in the deep woods, the long absence from home, the association with lesser characters and the arduous work in the waist-deep snow resulted in a desire for excitement, freedom and liquor which few men could resist.

At the closing of the camps some of the married men took train for home and family. Others, less resolute could get by the first saloon safely and perhaps the second but perhaps never get as far as the railway station to buy a ticket before they were completely broke.

Some of the men would get their camp time orders cashed, then deposit most of their winter's wages with some bartender, storekeeper or boarding house head, with instructions to deal it out in small sums on demand. Saloon keepers were the most avaricious of the lot. Lumberjacks were often surprised to learn from their "confidential" friend behind the bar that they had drawn out their entire stake of a hundred dollars or more within a week. Conscience played no major role with the men in the white apron.

Woodsmen who spent their long winters in the camps would run through their little pile within a few days or weeks in town. Then, if they could, would run up bills for board, lodging and drink while waiting for the spring log drive down the Fox or the Driggs Rivers. When the drive was completed the same process left them in debt and again they awaited the call for crews for the next winter's work in the camps.

When the camp foreman needed a crew he would make the rounds of the boarding houses, saloons and stores, "stand good" for each man's bill to be taken out of his wages. So with his season's pay mortgaged, the jack packed his "turkey" and was off for another turn at camp life, with time to think over his past and to form new good resolutions.

Should a traveling preacher hold services in the bunkhouse during the winter, firm resolutions were again made, only to be broken in the majority of cases when town was struck again.

At every camp there were men in their latter years of life, men not old in anniversaries but aged by hard, rugged work and hard drinking, men who had lost their lusty manhood, burned out, old before their time, now fit only for stable boys, chore boys, camp cook helpers and "road monkeys," leisurely repenting a misspent life. The tragedies in the lives of these men seemed to be inseperably linked with the passing of the pine.

Indomitable as they seemed, the jacks' indomitableness was because of brawn rather than brain but their simple honesty and concern toward their fellow-workers underlay their best moments. They fought at "the drop of a hat;" they drank, gambled, caroused in every way. They worked long and hard for low wages and rough meals only to spend it all in a few hectic days. They gathered before the rough bars of the tinsel-bedecked, sawdust-floored saloons where they drank whiskey like water.

Men matured early in those days. Many a boy of fourteen began work in the woods as a teamster, handling a pair of big Percherons or Belgians, skidding logs from the place they were felled to the skidways, from which the timber was drawn on sleighs to the rollways to the river banks. Within a few years these youngsters blossomed forth into full-fleldged lumberjacks—real he-men of the woods, men of brawn and endurance such as have never been surpassed in the annals of American pioneering.

Notwithstanding the uneven course of the life they led—the rugged work in the deep snow and below-zero temperatures, the weeks of dissipation in town, the months of idleness when their stake was spent—despite these extremes of existence, many of these men lived to

CONTRACT CUTTERS AND CABIN

Small contractors undertook to cut pine at a set price per thousand and lived with their crews in isolated cabins.

U. of Mich. School of Natural Resources.

ripe old age. Today these few can be seen on the streets of Seney, Marquette, Manistique, Escanaba and dozens of Upper Peninsula towns, still dressed in their stagged pants, their plaid mackinaws, greasy hats and high-top boots, standing before the taverns with their cronies of a past era, engaged in reminiscences of by-gone days— most of them now living on old age pensions.

Dissipation of the early lumberjacks was keen amusement. Modernation was a word unknown to them. Though they were hardy to the highest possible degree, they never could have run the gamut of strong drink as they did and emerge unharmed but for their outdoor environment during the winter months. The clean, pure air in the wide open spaces in the resin-scented pine woods served to rejuvenate them and their regular hours of sleep and the coarse but nourishing food built for them constitutions of iron.

The old-time lumberjack did thoroughly what he had to do. He put his whole heart into his work and his play, into his sleeping and his sporting. He had a rough exterior and a heart of gold. He could out-drink, out-work and out-sport men of other occupations. He went about his activities lustily, with pride in his accomplishments. He bragged loudly in camp and in town about the record cut in the woods, the champion load of logs drawn to the rollways by the camp's prize team of horses, the amount of whiskey he could drink and the fights he had engaged in.

To the man who treated him fairly and gave him a square deal or true friendship, he was a square dealer and a true friend. If he felt himself agrieved, and he often acquired that feeling when drinking, he took no devious ways to adjust the matter. He went directly after physical satisfaction—with fists, boot-calks and sometimes teeth in action. The Marquis of Queensbury, who developed the rules of our man-to-man fighting practises, would have found much to criticize as a witness to the typical lumberjack fight, but he would have seen some real fights. He would have seen no mixing in, no interference from the sidelines. It was "mind your own business" and let the fight go on, "let the best man win." The rule was enforced with compensation for its obedience and definite penalties for its infraction. The participant who had had enough could say so, acknowledge himself beaten, with no "face losing" except what might have been chipped off by the calks of his opponent's boots. The next time he might well be the victor. Until he realized himself bettered in the fight, he could, and willingly did, carry on. The methods and practises did not differ appreciably from those of modern warfare, but no time was lost in calling the rules "civilized" while the argument was going on. Only results counted. The end justified the means. Knives were seldom used. When they were, the onlookers stopped the fight, took away the lethal weapon, then pushed the adversaries back into the circle to finish it out with bare fists. Only the personal weapons with which the men were born, plus the calked boot, were allowed. Anything else was looked upon as being outside the code.

CHAPTER FIVE

Christmas At Seney

It was Christmas time at Seney. Lumberjacks and foremen with families generally took a week's vacation to spend the holiday with them. A number of the single men, who remembered their boyhood celebrations at home, were invited to join these families.

It was during this short vacation that Dr. F. P. Bohn was kept busy. His own holiday was all together given over to the disputants in lumberjack arguments—arguments intended to adjust a previous grievance or just to settle the question as to which was the better man. These jousts could be followed to the doctor's office by the red trails they left, trails that reddened and broadened as the day wore on.

The wild woodsmen were in for a holiday of relaxation from the monotony of the lumber camps, in to celebrate, in to give release to the boundless energies which their robust manhood and their vigorous camp life had generated. The twenty-one or more drinking places in Seney had abundant incentives for the controversies the ardent, lusty he-men from the woods indulged in. Extra supplies of hard liquor had been brought in for the occasion. It was not, therefore, wholly in the Christmas spirit, as that spirit, of brotherly love is traditionally understood, that the impressive guests from the backwoods regions celebrated their holiday.

The most marked and constant feature of the day and the nights before and after, indicated that brotherly love was absent and that peace on earth was gone and forgotten. It was in these times and after the breakup of the camps in the spring that Seney acquired the reputation which made it possible for the pilgrim who journeyed thither merely to ask the ticket agent in any neighboring town for "a ticket to hell" and be sure of being sold a ticket to Seney.

When the celebration was at its height long standing feuds broke out between the personnel of rival lumber camps. These usually started when an inebriated man began to boast of the millions of feet of pine cut in his camp, the great load of logs hauled on one sleigh to the river bank, or who was the champion fighter of all the camps. Each camp had its prize bully or "bull-of-the-woods" who could lick any other bully with one hand tied behind his back. As these arguments grew hotter and hotter, a local camp champion was pushed into the middle of the sawdust-covered floor of the saloon where he challenged the best of them all. He did not have long to wait until a rival gang shoved their man into the ring and the fight was on.

As one fight was finished and the victor declared, the rival crews moved to the bar and the feud declared at an end until the next celebration. No grudges lasted beyond the last drink.

The holiday ended, the men went back to camp, some broke, some scarred with "lumberjack smallpox" from a kick in the face by a calked boot, to gather again when the next Christmas rolled around.

In the meantime all was not riot in other parts of Seney. Families gathered around their warm living rooms to sing Christmas carols and to exchange gifts. The little church on the corner held its Christmas Eve program of "pieces" spoken in droning voices by the children, the big spruce tree loaded with tinsel, strung popcorn and red cranberries and a bright angel at the top. Santa Claus did not forget the youngsters in this far away land, for he came through the wide church door at the proper moment with his pack of toys, paper sacks filled with nuts and candy and oranges to distribute these meager treats to the excited children, some of whose fathers were celebrating in another fashion in Dan Dunn's saloon.

CHAPTER SIX

A Day In A Lumber Camp

THE PRINCIPLE LUMBER COMPANIES about Seney paid little for their stands of pine as compared with timber price of today. The prevailing price for an acre of giant White and Norway pine, which stood so thickly that sunlight rarely reached the ground, was $1.25. Between $40.00 to $60.00 was the average cost of forty acres of standing timber. At today's price it would have cost them around $10,500.00.

Lumber syndicates in Boston, New York and Chicago bought great areas of pine land from the land office and the railroads, the latter having acquired it for the price of extending their lines between the Soo and Escanaba and from Manistique and Marquette. It was the practise of some of the companies to buy sections of timber land, then extend their cuttings into surrounding timber which they did not own, "round sections or forties," these were called.

While fortunes were made for distant owners the lumberjacks received a pitifully small portion of it. The men who did the actual labor received from $25.00 to $30.00 a month with meals and a straw-covered bunk to sleep in, provided they stayed the season through. A deduction of $2.00 per month was made by some of the companies if a man quit before the spring breakup. This

35

was done to keep the men from roaming from one camp to another and disrupting the work crew and slowing up production.

River drivers were paid on the average of $2.00 a day, for their work was not only more hazardous but the working conditions were more rugged, with icy water and slippery logs and the hours stretched from twelve to fourteen, with long walks back to the moving camp site in addition.

Teamsters had their own scale of wages and their own time schedule through the winter season, measured by the daylight possibilities. Their pay ranged from $35.00 to $45.00 a month and their work started at three or four in the morning with the feeding of their horses, the grooming and harnessing before the other men were out of their bunks. Some men drove teams on the sprinkler sleighs at night to sprinkle water on the hauling roads to make them slippery with ice for the great loads of logs hauled over them. There was pride in the size of the load of logs a team could haul and each teamster cared for his horses as though they were his precious children to keep them in good condition for their strenuous work.

The non-air conditioned bunkhouses were built of logs and chinked with mud and moss from the swamps. Rough board bunks, two or three tiers high, were set around three walls, filled with straw from the horsebarn and covered with heavy woolen blankets supplied by the company. A great horizontal stove stuffed with four foot lengths of hardwood heated the place. Above the stoves were lines of haywire on which the men dried their socks, wet mackinaws and mittens during the weeks and their

THE CAMP COOK AND COOKEE
The Cook's word was law in the cook shack. He was either friend
or tyrant to the crew. Good cooking meant contented and happy
lumberjacks.

Burton Historical Collections.

washing on Sundays. A skylight in the roof let out the strong odor of the sweating, smoking men and the smell of drying clothes. Some of the old lumberjacks contended that night air was poisonous and insisted that the skylight be kept closed.

The cookhouse was the chief institution in the camps. Built of logs from the surrounding woods, it served both as kitchen and dining room and had a small leanto attached to house the cook. Here the staples were beans and tea. The lumberjack's choice was bean soup. Those old camp cooks knew how to prepare it too. Michigan could never have been logged off and cleared for settlement without beans. Beans and tea were served every meal. It was green tea and strong enough to float an ax. Its strength fitted the strength of the hardy men who poured it down their throats, boiling hot as it came off the cook's stove. Beans, tea and Peerless tobacco were the trinity without which no lumber camp could operate.

There were other varieties of good, wholesome food, well cooked, strongly flavored, satisfying and filling, on the menu. Those who refer to the old river driver as the supreme example of lumberjack ability have overlooked what that bully-boy could and did regularly do when he seated himself, placed both elbows on the board table in the cookhouse and began refueling himself for the energy to be expended on the day's work in the woods.

On the table at breakfast were stewed prunes (considered a "regulator"), beans, tea, fried potatoes, pie, cake, cookies, doughnuts, bread, oleomargarine and a variety of other food calculated to stick to the ribs of even a rugged jack.

The noon meal in the woods, served up by the camp

cookee from the one-horse jumper drawn to the scene of the cutting, consisted of all the above items plus hot beef stew, all of which was quickly inhaled by the hungry men who came back for seconds and thirds.

The supper back in camp, eaten long after darkness had stopped the work in the woods, was of the same variety, with some special pie or pudding.

Silence in the cookhouse was a ritual rigidly observed and strictly enforced by the cook. Any newcomer who started a conversation was ignored by his fellows. If that did not suffice, he felt vigorous kicks under the table. Should that be insufficient to silence him, the cook took a hand and ordered him to be quiet or get out. Cooks had work to do and conversation delayed them and the overworked cookees. So silence to them was golden.

The van or camp store managed by the camp clerk was stocked with a supply of lumberjack necessities—tobacco, snuff, mittens, socks, shirts, mackinaws, rubber and leather boots and caps. No liquor was sold. Here at the van the men could buy on a charge account against their wages.

The log cook shacks of the lumber camps were busy places. The alarm clock rang madly and the cook opened his eyes long before the dawn had begun to filter through the little window of his leanto bedroom. He shouted at the cookee who soon had a roaring fire going in the two big cookstoves.

The long, oilcloth-covered tables were soon piled with food, with fifty or sixty places set at each table. The cook was busy stirring the pancake batter in fifty-pound lard cans. Clouds of smoke arose from the hot griddles and escaped through the open skylight in the roof. The cookee placed large pans of pork sausage in the oven. Sliced potatoes were dumped into enormous skillets and set on the hot stove.

The little, old wizened choreboy staggered in with two pails of water from the nearby spring. His former angelic nature had long since been warped by drink, quarreling with the jacks for spitting on his floor and having been made a scapegoat of numerous practical jokes. His treatment left a cranky, snarling, carping fox.

"Got any coffee, cook?" he yelled. "Bin up fer an hour waiting for your lazy cook crew to open up."

When the cook had several large cake tins piled high with pancakes, he called:

"Let 'er go, Pete. Git them timber savages outta bed!"

The chore boy took the "chuck horn" from the wall and going to the cookhouse door, he blew a long and doleful blast, a sound, which on a clear, cold winter's morning, could be heard for miles.

The sausage and potatoes, now golden brown, were placed on the tables. Steaming pots of green tea and coffee and mounds of flapjacks were lugged on.

"All set," came from the cook. "Let 'em have it."

The long benches were pulled out from the tables. Then at a second blast from the horn, the stampede began. Men of all descriptions and nationalities filed in, young men, old grizzled veterans, short and tall men, smiling, scowling. The foreman, the straw push, the bookkeeper and the scaler stalked to their places of state at the head of the nearest table. Except for an occasional cough, the creaking of the benches, the clatter of steel utensils on the tin plates, there was surprisingly little noise. The cookee was kept on the run. Dishes emptied with speed and gallons of tea and coffee disappeared down the burning throats of the men.

Within a few minutes the food was gone, the cookhouse empty but for the sweating cook and his helpers. The pastries and empty dishes were removed and the dishes bathed in boiling water on the stoves, then set to dry on the drainboard for the next meal. Preparations for the noon lunch came next. Then that restful task, potato peeling, began.

From the outside came the clanking of chains as great teams of horses were driven to their work. The blacksmith's anvil began its tatoo for the day. The crack of the chore boy's ax at the woodpile drifted in. The real work of the day had begun.

The cook began his baking, his arms bare, with shirt sleeves rolled high, his hands deep in the bread dough. By the time the dough was kneaded and set in the racks behind the cookstove to raise, the cookee had two bushels of potatoes peeled.

"Let Pete and Joe finish the spuds," ordered the cook. "Cut out them eyes. Sam, grease these bread pans. How's the cake? Holdin' out? No cake today? Give 'em rice pudding with raisins for supper. Baking comes this morning, so we'll scrub the floor this afternoon. Pies to be out first. An' the beggies got to be peeled. No foolin' today, boys."

CHAPTER SEVEN

Preparing For Supper

LUMBER CAMPS were supplied with heavy steer or "block" bull beef. The meat was cut into large pieces and placed in large covered boilers the day before it was served. It was covered with water and allowed to simmer and slowly boil until nine o'clock the next day. Then it was removed from the boilers, placed in large pans, covered with the broth and baked in the oven to brown until the other food was ready to serve. This process assured the men of tender, juicy meat for supper.

Bushels of potatoes were set to boil on the back of the stove. One of the cookees peeled rhutabeggas while the chore boy swept and mopped the kitchen floor. The cook rolled and stamped out hundreds of cookies and baked them on flat pans. In one hour there were enough cookies in the big lard cans to last the crew for three days.

Forty circles of doughnuts were placed on a floured board and dumped all at once into a big kettle of hot bacon grease. By nine o'clock the baking was finished.

There was whistling and commotion outside the kitchen door. The grimy face of the blacksmith appeared through the opening.

"Brother, I smelt them fried cakes clear out in my shop," he smiled as he stuffed his pocket with the hot cakes.

If the crew were working near the camp several dropped in casually to get a handout during the morning. At eleven o'clock the dinner horn brought them in. The tables were ready. The smell of boiled cabbage, carrots and rhutabeggas and the frying doughnuts filled the cook shack and drifted out of the door. The brisk air had done its work and the men appeared famished. There were stragglers, too—jacks who had drifted in for work, some only for a meal on their way to other camps. They stood at the door until the crew was seated and the cookees found empty places for them. No man was ever turned away. Night lodging in the bunkhouse was given these floaters if the end of the day found them in the camp. After a hearty breakfast they were on their way to seek work or just a few free meals.

One stranger, evidently new to camp life, tried to strike up a conversation with his neighbor at the table. The cook regarded him ominously for a while, then walked the length of the eating place and tapped him roughly on the shoulder.

"No talkin' at the table, partner."

The white apron and the inevitable white cap were badges of authority and the fellow said no more.

The storm of another meal was over and the wreck cleared away. The benches were piled on the tables and scrubbing began. The cookees wielded the brooms while the chore boy swept the surplus soapy water into convenient cracks and knotholes in the floor. By now heavy snores came from the direction of the cook's bedroom. The chore boy growled and grumbled as he carried more water from the creek. He saw no reason for scrubbing more than twice a week. It just made more work. The

MEALS UNDER KEROSENE LAMPS

The woods crew saw daylight in the camps only on Sunday. Up before dawn and back after dark, they had little leisure or recreation.

Burton Historical Collections.

place would only get dirty again.

Before the scrubbing was finished, the supply team arrived. The teamster carried in boxes of canned goods, a barrel of sausage, quarters of beef, whole hog carcasses, sacks of flour, boxes of dried prunes and raisins and that staple without which no camp could operate—cases of tobacco, especially Peerless. It was a common saying that Peerless was never wasted. The lumberjacks smoked it, chewed it, snuffed it in powder form, then blew their noses and greased their boots.

The balance of the afternoon was the time for the kitchen boys and the chore boy to relax and rest. Some climbed into their bunks and were soon fast asleep. One sat in his bunk in the dim light which came through the skylight reading the latest copy of his dime novel, Nick Carter, Master Detective.

With most of the food prepared in the morning, supper meant less effort. The left-overs from the noon meal were supplemented by a batch of hot baking powder biscuits or johnny cake. After the dishes were washed, the tables set for breakfast, the morning bacon sliced, the cook crew went into the big bunkhouse, all except the cook. His station demanded that he stay with the ship.

Some of the jacks were already in bed, snoring. Many were playing cards. Others gathered before the "deacon's seat" listening to an old-timer spinning yarns of the tall timber, with stories about Ho-dogs, Paul Bunyan, Johnny Inkslinger and snowsnakes. Several young fellows were propped in their bunks reading the pink Police Gazette and western novels. There was a rancid odor of drying socks, tarpaper, melting shoe grease and pine pitch as the big stove in the middle of the room became hotter. Through it all came the soft strains of a guitar from a far corner and the voice of the player rendering "The Red Light Saloon."

The weazened chore boy limped in and called:—

"Quarter past nine! Lights out!"

Another day in the lumber camp had passed into history.

The camps in the early days supplied little fresh meat for the crews. Their steady diet of "red-horse" (pickled beef), dry and salt pork became monotonous. Deer became scarce in winter because the deep snow prevented the poachers from going out to find fresh meat on the hoof, so the occasional venison stew was missing. After weeks of this diet of "embalmed" meat, the men at headquarters Camp Seven up the Fox River decided to take the matter into their own hands.

They cast their eyes at the herd of large, fat hogs which was owned by the company and fed the rich garbage thrown out by the cook. These hogs would be shipped to Chicago packing houses in the spring and sold for a good price. The men lured a large hog into the woods and killed and skinned it. They cut off the legs and head and told the cook that they had shot a fine, fat swamp bear which had come out of hibernation.

The cook prepared the fresh meat and was serving it to the men when Tom Millen, the walking boss, came in from his visit to some of the outlying camps. Tom, as chief push, was responsible for all the camp property. He joined the men at the head table and remarked how good swamp bear tasted.

"I hope you boys will keep your eyes peeled for another bear. It sure is good."

47

"I seed the tracks of one in the lower cuttings near the river," remarked Jerry Mahoney, the tote teamster, winking his eye at Mike Ross, who had thought of the scheme.

The boys who were in the know said nothing. A few weeks later word spread around that Millen would be away for several days. That night the men brought in two more swamp bear to the delight of the cook, who prepared a special meal of the meat, prune pie and fresh camp baked bread.

The men were jubilant at the tables, for they all now knew the source of this new treat. The cook shack burst open and in walked Boss Millen for a meal. There was an unusual silence at supper that evening. Eyes rolled toward the walking boss who seemed to be engrossed in his food, looking at it, tasting it but with little relish.

After supper Millen made a tour of the camp counting hogs. He returned within a few minutes and advised the crew and cook that they would have to dispense with swamp bear thereafter.

Oxen were used in some of the camps to skid logs out of the woods to the skidway. One ox had become temporarily crippled and was fattening in the barn on timothy and corn. When the critter had reached a desired state of corpulance, an "accident" occurred. One of the jacks had let it out and it wandered into the woods where the men were cutting trees. A carefully felled tree crashed down on it and broke its back. The camp had fresh meat for a week or more.

When the meat was gone, another ox met with a freak accident. The men carefully spaced these accidents far enough apart not to raise the suspicion of the woods boss.

The employees of the company at the Manistique mill,

DOCILE OXEN SKIDDED LOGS OUT OF THE WOODS
In deep snow these patient animals excelled horses.

Burton Historical Collections.

who roomed and boarded at the company boarding house, heard about those accidents. They, too, were tired of sowbelly and red horse. There was an ox in the company barn. It received unusual attention from the men and waxed fat.

One Sunday morning Jim Norton and "Ruffian" O'-Brien picked up a sledge hammer and a horseshoe with sharp calks protruding at the heel and toe and went into the barn to operate on the fatted ox. O'Brien tied the horseshoe over the critter's head, between the eyes. Norton swung the sledge hammer against the shoe and the ox dropped.

Very much excited over the fate of the animal, the two men rushed to report to the mill boss, Pat Murphy, that one of the horses in the barn had kicked the ox between the eyes. Murphy hurried out to the stable and saw with his own eyes the tragedy which had befallen the valuable animal.

Looking the ox over more closely, the boss exclaimed with a twinkle in his Irish blue eyes:

"Sure, enough, the animal is dead. You know, there's a funny thing about all this. The horseshoe mark is upside down. Aither the ox or the horse was laying on his back when the poor baste was kicked."

CHAPTER EIGHT

Wild Men From The Woods

Whan the lumberjacks came down from the camps to Seney in the spring with their hard-earned pay checks, they usually lost no time getting to the nearest saloon. Here they could meet their old cronies from the other camps and indulge in social rounds of treating and drinking.

Naturally, many drank more than they could handle easily. It was then one saw them in a different light. Some, when intoxicated, became happy as larks, singing and shouting as they staggered down the plank sidewalks or gave exhibitions of step-dancing on the barroom floors. Others displayed an opposite disposition. They became mean and ugly and set out looking for trouble. Some developed crying jags, chiding others for some fancied wrong, such as the refusal to take another drink with them. Strong drink often caused some to resolve to lead better lives in the future. These good intentions seldom lasted longer than the jag.

Sandy Morrison staggered into the general store and asked for a revolver to kill a man down the street. Bellaire refused to sell him one. C. E. Morse, one of the owners, winked at Bellaire and told him to sell him the one they had in the desk drawer. It was a 38 caliber without a firing pin, so Bellaire sold it to him at a nominal price.

Sandy then wanted a box of cartridges, but Bellaire was afraid that one might go off accidently, resulting in the death or injury of his adversary. Morse advised him to sell the wild man of the wood the loads. Sandy then asked Bellaire to load the chambers, then handed the clerk the remaining cartridges and a five dollar bill, remarking that he had enough cartridges to do the job.

He started down the street, walked up to his intended victim and began to snap the gun under his nose. The fellow dodged, but when he saw that the gun did not fire, he turned on Sandy, knocked him down and gave him a good beating. Sandy was laid up for a week. When he had recovered he came into the store and told Bellaire that he was thankful to him for selling him a worthless gun. He said that he had been drinking heavily and was insane enough to have killed the man.

"I want to thank you for your kindness. If that gun had worked, I would be serving time in some prison by now."

Bellaire returned the five dollars to him. That was the last time he saw Sandy under the influence of liquor.

One noon a drunken lumberjack came into the dining room of a local hotel for dinner and seated himself at the tables reserved for the rougher patrons, separate from those of the more elite boarders. When he had finished his meal he started out of the dining room by way of the kitchen door. The waitress tried to tell him he was going out the wrong door. He insisted that that was the door by which he came in.

"By God, if that is the right door, then you turned the hotel around since I came in."

The big, strong woman who presided in the kitchen helped him out of the kitchen door with a substantial kick which sent him outdoors faster than he had come in.

Some jacks liked to yell at the top of their voices when they felt the effects of John Barleycorn. They would drag their mackinaws down the street by one hand and waving their caps in the other, shouting:

"I'm a bad man in a small town! I'm a wolf! I'm a bear! I kin lick any man who walks down the streets of Seney!"

Generally these wild men were promptly accommodated.

On Saturday nights the storekeeper made up his weekly bills and sent young Bellaire to make the rounds of the saloons to collect them. The clerk had entered one saloon just as one of the boys had thrown a ten dollar bill on the bar and ordered the bartender to give all the men a drink. The barkeep asked Bellaire to wait a minute for his money. The clerk stepped behind the end of the bar to be out of the way as the men rushed up.

The bartender lined up mugs of beer on the front of the mahogany. The men had just come in fresh from the drive and wore their calked boots. As they crowded at the bar one of the men stepped an another's foot and the calks bit deeply. The injured man emitted a yell and an oath and struck the offender a hard blow in the face. The latter's chum struck back with a sledge hammer fist that laid the clumsy driver low. In less time than it would take to tell it the entire gang was smashing and tearing at each other like a pack of wolves.

The bartender bounded over the bar onto the sawdust

covered floor and cleared it of fighting men as quickly as the fight had started. Then laughing to Bellaire, he paid the clerk his bill and went about his business as if nothing unusual had happened.

One stocky woodsman just released from his winter's job stepped off the train at Seney "feeling his oats." He jumped into the air and shouted at the crowd at the station:

"I kin lick any man who walks the streets of Seney."

No one paid any attention to him. He kept shouting and getting louder. As he passed a saloon, powerfully built Tim Kaine stepped out on the walk, looked up at the approaching "wolf of the woods," winked at the men nearby and stepped into the path of the approaching jack. As the man started to yell his challenge again, Kaine's arm shot out and the fighting man tumbled into the muddy street. He had found what he was looking for. When he picked himself up, one eye was closed and the other was closing. The crowd walked away to see what other excitement might be happening on the streets of wild and wide open Seney.

Although Seney had its numerous lumberjack fights when the men came into town to cash their pay slips, there were times between when the village inhabitants lived a monotonous existence. In the camps life was oftentimes a continuous round of working, eating and sleeping during the hard, long, cold winters. In town these dull times, however, were sometimes brightened by the telling of tall tales. The saloons and the general stores were the scenes of story telling, enriched by fabulous tales of accomplishments in the woods, yarns of heroic deeds done in far away places, experiences with the law and lewd women. The big heating stoves in the stores and taverns warmed up bodies as well as imaginations.

Another diversion in this backwoods community life was the playing of practical jokes which everyone but the victims enjoyed. Seney had its quota of practical jokers who hesitated at nothing.

If anyone enjoyed a practical joke, it was Horace Shorter, the engineer on the Manistique railroad running from Manistique to Grand Marais on Lake Superior. The Morse & Schneider store always had a pair of cats which had free range of the place and were more effective than traps to keep down the mice and rat population.

It was near Christmas time. Among the various items displayed in the store was a quantity of candle holders which were used to snap onto the branches of Christmas trees with strong springs. One noon R. E. Schneider was trying to wait on some women customers but was disturbed by the antics of the cats, which raced about the store, jumped onto the groceries, yowling and spitting. They acted like drunken lumberjacks. Schneider called Bellaire to open the door and either catch the cats or get them out of the store.

Shorter sat by the heating stove innocently watching the crazy cats. He made no attempt to help Bellaire, who finally succeeded in catching one of the cats. Examining it, he found one of the steel snaps fastened to the end of its tail. What Schneider said to Shorter was not fit for ladies' ears. The stunt gave Shorter an idea. He bought some of the candle holders and put them in his mackinaw pocket.

On his way home he stopped for a visit at Mike Ryan's boarding house. The dining room and sitting room were one. The tables were near the window, loaded with dishes and covered by cheesecloth, to keep off the dust. Mrs. Ryan's pet tom cat jumped upon Shorter's knee and nestled in his lap for a comfortable nap. Suddenly it emitted a desperate yowl, plunged over the dish-loaded table and dived through the window, breaking the glass in his mad lunge.

Everyone was greatly surprised by the strange antics of the old family mouser. The family ran out of doors and found the cat buried in the deep snow, clawing at the clamp on his tail. They all descended upon Shorter and demanded an apology and payment for the broken dishes and window pane. Mrs. Ryan led him back to the store, selected a new set of dishes and ordered the window pane replaced. The bill came to over five dollars which the practical joker gladly paid, saying:

"The fun was worth the price!"

A harmless figure was Andy Daly, known as "Buck." He delighted in going up and down the street shouting:—

"Romeo, you snowflake! Come out of the wet, you savage!"

He would shout so loud that he could be heard all over the little town. A Detroit clothing salesman was carrying his sample cases from the depot. As he passed Dunn's saloon, Daly came up behind him and let out a whoop which could have wakened the dead. The salesman, taken by surprise, dropped his cases, tripped over them and fell off the high wooden walk into the ditch. Daly was not intoxicated—just having a little fun at the expense of the city drummer.

On another occasion Daly was walking down the sidewalk carrying a large bundle of oat straw to "Daddy"

O'Brien's cow. As he passed in front of the White House Hotel, some bystander remarked:—

"What a good stunt it would be to set fire to that straw and have some fun with that joker."

It was no sooner suggested than a native slipped up behind Daly, set fire to the straw and dodged back. The flames rushed over the bundle. Daly let out a shout of surprise and threw the straw into the street and ran, holding his backsides.

One spring a sick and accident insurance agent sold about twenty-five policies to the local people at the cost of one dollar a month, payable in advance. Bellaire was appointed collector. An old Irishman named Finnigan was choring at the White House Hotel for Tom Harcourt and took out a policy, which stated in bold print that in the event of sickness or accident he was to receive a percentage of his monthly wages for medical service and medicine.

Everything went along nicely for a few months. The men paid Bellaire and no one had an accident or was sick. Finnigan continued his work at Harcourt's hotel, cared for and milked the cow stabled in a small barn on the back of the hotel lot.

It had been a long, hard, cold winter. The snow was four feet deep on the level. The cow had not been out of the barn and in the open air all winter long. On the first warm spring day Harcourt asked his chore boy to tie a rope to the cow's horns and take her out for a little exercise and fresh air.

Finnigan dutifully tied one end of the rope about the critter's horns and the other end around his own wrist. He opened the barn door. The cow came slowly out into the warm spring air and sunshine. She looked about, then started down the street with a bound, pulling the little Irishman along. He could not keep up the swift pace set by the cow and soon lost his footing on the slippery snow, yelling for help with the little breath left in him. People came out of the saloons and stores to see what the new commotion was about. There was poor Finnigan dangling from the end of the rope, swinging from one side of the street to the other, plowing a deep furrow in the snow as he slid along.

The crowd caught the cow as soon as she became exhausted by her gay gallop and untied Finnigan from his critter. He could barely walk without help. They led him to the hotel and put him in bed. Dr. W. W. French was called to bind up the rope burns. It was several days before the chore boy was able to resume his work.

Bellaire, as the insurance collector, filed a claim with his company. The company wrote back that the insured was not insured against any accident which occurred to the policyholder from tying himself to a wild cow, but under the circumstances they would allow him something for his unfortunate accident. After the doctor's bill was paid and the doctor's report was filed, Finnigan had just enough left for the price of two mugs of beer, which he bought and drank. That ended the accident insurance organization in Seney.

Paddy Joice had come down to Seney from his winter's work in the camps and spent his money on whiskey and women until he was flat broke. He begged all the drinks he could from his fellow workers but soon ran out of friends. Thirsty and hungry he went to the town pump to get a drink of water. He worked the pump handle fruitlessly for several minutes, not knowing that the pump needed priming. Finally giving up, he was heard to remark:

"I don't blame you for not giving me a drink of water. I come to you only when I'm broke."

Free lunches were always placed at the end of the saloon bars in order to keep the drinkers from leaving to secure a meal. Rye bread, salty pretzels, cheeses of all kinds, ranging from mild American to odorous limburger, pickles and salted herring. Though beer sold for five cents a glass, the saloon keeper made his profit from straight whiskey. The lunch, reserved only for steady customers, was an investment in good will.

One winter day a number of the logging company officials came in on the D.S.S. & A. train, among them an Englishman whose family had a financial interest in the logging business. The Britain dressed in his tweeds, an ulster and a cane, looked about him curiously as the men stopped in at the first saloon for a "shot." After a round of drinks, the bartender invited them to have a snack of lunch at the end of the bar. It was a new experience to the foreigner, who asked the bartender to make him up a sandwich. The bartender obligingly cut two slices of rye bread and placed a chunk of limburger cheese between them and handed it to the Englishman. He looked at it, smelled it, took a bite, then spit it out and threw the sandwich onto the sawdust-covered floor. As the men circled round to watch the performance, the ever present saloon cat walked between their legs, sniffed at the sandwich, then proceeded to cover it with sawdust. The Englishman watched for a minute, then remarked:

"I thought so."

CHAPTER NINE

The Mail Went Through

T HE SENEY POSTOFFICE was established in the winter of 1883. John F. Chisholm was the first postmaster. Others followed during the lumber days—Tom Millen, W. W. Hargrave, R. E. Schneider, then Hargrave again, to be succeeded by John I. Bellaire who held the office during the administrations of Presidents William McKinley, Theodore Roosevelt and William Howard Taft, until the spring of 1904. One of the first rural mailcarriers was R. E. Schneider, a partner in the Morse & Schneider General Store. He was succeeded by Jock Delong who carried on through the logging days.

The lumber companies charged each man ten cents a month to have his mail carried in. The carrier made round trips throughout the various camps twice a month. This arrangement was satisfactory to the crews and kept them satisfied. It also forstalled the men going to town for their mail and staying on a protracted spree before they returned.

The mail carrier was given the right to buy items the men wanted and deliver them for a small charge. This charge and the ten cents from each man in the camp for his mail delivery amounted to a good monthly income for the carrier.

At the Seney postoffice letters were received from many

parts of the United States and some from foreign countries—from mothers, husbands, wives, sweethearts and friends of the boys in the forest whom they were trying to locate. Officers of the law at times wrote to the postmaster for information concerning individuals trying to evade the law. A number of men took refuge in the woods camps of the area. In most cases the postmaster was able to render valuable assistance in the search, for he had the list of names of the men working in all the camps and had met or seen most of them as they appeared in town or in the Morse & Schneider store where the post-office was located.

One winter as Bellaire was distributing the mail and filling the mail bags for delivery to the camps, a U. S. marshall from the state of New York came in, displayed his star and other credentials of identification. He was looking for a defaulting cashier who had disappeared twenty years before. He stated that the authorities had traced every rumor and clew without success thus far. Finally they began to search the lumber camps, especially those in the out of the way places, where their man might have holed up.

The marshall had found traces of his man in the camps in and around Peshitigo, Wisconsin, and Menominee, Michigan. As a last resort they decided to try Seney where fifteen lumber companies were operating and were the rendezvous of a number of questionable characters.

After being assured that he was within his legal rights in assisting the officer, Bellaire searched through the various camp mailing lists. He knew many of the men personally and was able to furnish a description of some of them. The hunted man had many aliases but he found one who seemed to answer the officer's description. He had cashed his camp time slip at the store several times. Bellaire had noticed him particularly and had wondered why he was working as a common laborer in a logging camp. His hand-writing was good, not like that of most of the other men, some of whom could sign their slips with only a cross. It was reasoned that he must have been well educated, that he had possibly had some misfortune, had fallen from grace and sought the isolation of the camps as a hide-out from friends and relatives. He had mingled little with the other men and always held his own council.

With this information the marshall set off to the camp and next day returned with his man. When they entered the store the officers told his man that he would not have to work in the lumber camps for a long time to come. The prisoner shook hands with Bellaire and thanked him for the good treatment he had received from him over the months since he had come to Seney. He said he was happy it was over and was ready to go back to face the charges. He had spent and squandered the stolen money and had been living in fear for many years. He had eyed every stranger whom he had met, fearing that he might be an officer searching for him.

Many farm boys from the Lower Peninsula came north in the fall to work in the camps and returned home in the spring to put in their crops. These young men were mostly sober and saving individuals. They came into the Morse & Schneider store in the spring, bought enough items to assist in cashing their time slips, then filled out money orders for the balance except for a small amount for food and the price of a ticket to take them across the car ferry operating between St. Ignace and Mackinaw City. The money orders they mailed in envelopes addressed to themselves in their home town and deposited them on the U. S. Mail.

Bellaire asked one of the young men why he took this precaution and he replied:—

"It will be there when I get there. I can't spend it and I'll need every cent when I start farming this spring. No one can rob me. I can bum a ride on the freight train to St. Ignace but not on the ferry."

One lumberjack came into the postoffice, bought a stamp, placed it on the envelope he had someone address for him and deposited it in the mail chute. He stood around a few minutes, then turned to the postmaster, saying:

"I suppose it is there now."

"Where?"

"To where I sent it."

He knew that when he mailed a letter in the post office it always went to the place addressed but he did not know how or by what means it traveled.

Another woodsman came into the store, somewhat excited, and wanted to know if Bellaire was the postmaster.

"I'm glad I found you in," he said in a hushed voice. "I came to you for protection. There is a crowd down the street wanting to kill me. If you'll protect me and save my life, I'm worth $50,000.00 and I'll give it all to you."

The postmaster sensed that the man was "not right." He did not look as though he was worth five cents. Bellaire humored him and assured him that no harm would come to him. That seemed to please him and he quieted down.

Shortly thereafter William Seeley, the railroad telegraph operator, came in for the out-going mail. Bellaire told the lumberjack that he would have to sack up the mail but that Seeley would protect him while he was in the back room. In a few seconds pandemonium broke loose in the store. Seeley called for Bellaire to come quickly—there was a madman loose!

As Bellaire came through the door he saw the wild man's eyes bulging with fear. He had an iron kettle in each hand and was looking for someone at whom to throw it. Seeley jumped behind the counter. As the fellow saw Bellaire he turned and threw one of the heavy kettles at him with all the force he had. Bellaire dodged and the kettle struck the door casing and caved it in. Then he threw the second kettle at Seeley, smashing the glass showcase and driving its contents behind the counter.

Seeley started to run for the back door, dodging kettles, canned goods and anything the crazed man would lay his hands on. The postmaster grabbed a canthook and tried to knock the man down. The latter whirled around and drove an iron kettle at him with all his might. Bellaire dodged the missile by inches. The kettle hit the front of the post office cabinet, broke the glass front and drove out several of the lock-boxes.

The mad man then ran out of the front door and down the plank sidewalk. Seeing a number of people coming to see what the commotion was all about, he ran back into the store. Bellaire dived at him and pinned his arms at his sides. The two went to the floor with a crash, with the fellow trying to bite his assailant. Bellaire called to a clerk to bring him a clothesline from a nearby counter.

He soon had plenty of help. They tied the man hand and foot and called Deputy Sheriff Jim Harcourt.

"What in hell were you trying to do?" asked the officer.

From the floor came the answer:

"I was doing the best I could but those damn fellows were too much for me."

Dr. F. P. Bohn was called and he advised Harcourt to get some whiskey which they poured down the man's throat. This quieted him but the deputy took no chances. He handcuffed the man and took him to his brother's saloon and placed him in a large arm chair to quiet down and rest, while Harcourt and the sheriff sat down to play a game of cards.

As the game was going on, someone shouted:

"Look out, Jim!"

The prisoner had sneaked up behind Harcourt and was in the act of bringing his handcuffs down on the deputy's head. The officer dodged but was struck on the head and shoulder by the handcuffs, which cut a deep gash in his right ear. Harcourt bounded out of his chair, grabbed the man and threw him into the arm chair with such force that it took all the fight out of him.

Harcourt then made his prisoner hold up his hands while he removed the metal bands, then forced him to put his hands behind him through the chair rungs and snapped the handcuffs on both wrists.

After an hour the man quieted down again and Harcourt took him to the White House Hotel and put him in bed, removed his handcuffs and set a man to watch over him. He caused no more trouble and was soon snoring peacefully.

Within a few days Harcourt led his man into the store, now sober and humble. He wanted to know if anyone was hurt in the melee and what damages he had caused. Bellaire assured him that he had hurt no one, which greatly relieved him. He agreed to pay for the broken glass, the crockery and the dented post office cabinet, which came to a total of fifteen dollars. There the matter was dropped—just "one of those things" in Seney.

It appeared that the man had been drinking very heavily for several days and had had an attack of delirium tremens and remembered nothing of the incident after he had sobered up at the hotel.

A few months after this happened the same lumberjack started working at Hugh Shay's shingle mill at Germfask, a village south of Seney, on the Manistique River. The mill employees boarded with the Edward Menere family, which operated a large boarding house. Twenty mill workers slept in one large room. The jack had another attack of tremens and attacked one of the sleeping men in his bed. The drunk had him by the throat with one hand and was striking him in the face with his fist. The sleeper bounded out of bed, knocked his attacker down, then lifted him up and threw him down the open stairway. The jack fell in a heap, knocked unconscious.

Within seconds several kerosene lamps were lighted and all the men were out of their rooms to see what was going on. Fortunately no bones were broken. The roomers interceded for the drunk, pointing out that the man was "out" for the night and could do no further harm. The men went downstairs to see how the man was faring. He remained unconscious until the next morning and did not recover from his ride down the stairway for two weeks.

He drew his time at the mill and left for other, less rugged places, never to return to Seney.

Letters came to the Seney postoffice at times with only the addressee's name and "Michigan, United States of America" on the envelope. When such letters from a foreign country arrived at the New York postoffice they were enclosed in an official envelope and addressed to the postmaster at Detroit. When the addressee could not be found in Detroit, the envelope was addressed:

"Try Postmaster, Seney, Michigan."

Then the Seney postmaster searched his lumber camp mailing list. Should the name be found, the letter was delivered by the camp mail carrier, who required the receiver to sign a receipt form to be mailed back to the Detroit postoffice.

However, many such letters never reached the addressee. Seney was at times the "port of missing men." Men killed in the lumber camps were buried in the little cemetery on the edge of Seney without a marker. Rivermen, drowned on the drive, were often interred by their fellow workers on the bank of the stream with only their calked boots hung on a nearby tree to mark their final resting place. How many others met their end in out of the way places, no one ever knew. Letters addressed to these missing men were returned to the "dead letter" department at Washington, D. C., and relatives never again heard from their men who were "killed in action" on the battle ground of the deep pine forest.

CHAPTER TEN

Tragedy in the Woods

EXTREME COLD and blinding blizzards forced undue hardship upon the hard working lumberjacks engaged in felling the pine and the townspeople during the early days in the north country.

There were no well-kept highways. The idea of snow removal had not yet been thought of. When the snow was deep on the sidewalks of Seney people merely walked in the roads smoothed down by the travel of horses and sleighs. In going from one lumber camp to another, the men followed narrow logging trails or just plunged into the trackless forest and made a bee line toward their destination, at times to their death. Many feet, hands and faces were severely frostbitten in the woods when the thermometer registered between the twenties and forties. It was not an uncommon occurrence for men to have to have their fingers and toes amputated after such exposure. Some lifeless forms of men lost in the blizzards were found days, weeks and sometimes months afterward.

One especially severe winter William Carr worked in Ed Cookson's camp north of Seney on the headwaters of the Driggs River when he received a letter advising him that he was the father of twin girls. Carr and his wife lived with her parents on the old Chicago Lumber Company farm eight miles southwest of the village of Germfask, near the mouth of the Driggs River. One of the worst northwest blizzards was raging at the time the letter reached him. The birth of the twins had occurred a week before the letter came.

No amount of persuasion or warning on the part of Carr's fellow workers could stop him from making the trip from the camp, over the swamps and through the thick forest to his wife and babies. He drew his time check and accompanied by another worker and left the camp the next morning, striking off into the woods by the shortest route.

In the face of the blizzard the men became separated and lost. Carr reached or stumbled by chance onto the track of the Manistique Logging Railroad southwest of Seney. Remaining on the track, he arrived safely at Germfask early in the morning, almost completely exhausted. The storm kept up. Several residents of Germfask urged him to stay in town all night, get a good sleep and start out the next morning when the storm may have expended itself. They assured him that his wife and children were getting along nicely and that in daylight he could travel faster and more safely. Angus McDougall, Germfask's only merchant and postmaster, invited him to stay with him overnight. He tried to warn Carr that it would be the height of folly and almost certain death to attempt the trip at night in the blinding storm.

Carr was determined to go on. His friends fed him well and loaned him more warm clothing and a pair of snowshoes.

He started out.

The men, who afterwards backtracked over the route

Carr had taken, found that he had made it through the woods to an open field within half a mile of the farm where his little family was sheltered. The deep, soft snow had prevented him from using the snowshoes. He had removed them. For a time he used them as crutches to assist him in fighting his way through the drifts to the fence which surrounded the farm. Here he had climbed over the rails, stumbled and fallen headfirst into the snow.

The next morning a neighbor woman, who was nursing Mrs. Carr and the twins, looked out of the window across the field and saw what appeared to be a body partly covered with snow, one arm held rigid over the snow. She waded through the drifts to a neighbor and together they dragged Carr's frozen body to his home. It was thought that he had become so exhausted in the blinding gale that he did not realize he was so close to his home and loved ones and had sunk into the snow where he had fallen.

Carr's companion had disappeared. Two years later Frank Aldo, a farmer near Seney, out looking for his cow, came upon the dry bones of a lumberjack on the east side of the small knoll in the swamp, only a few rods west of the railroad track onto which Carr had stumbled on his way to Germfask. Nothing had molested the body. From its position it appeared as if the fellow had become exhausted and laid down on the lee side of the knoll to rest. Sleep came with the numbing cold and nature did the rest. His clothing, socks, rubbers and mittens on his hands and the cap on his head were almost completely rotted away. There was nothing on or near the remains whereby it could be identified. The authorities made an investigation and concluded that the man was Carr's companion on that fatal walk.

CHAPTER ELEVEN

Danger on the Log Drives

THE WORK of the river-hog was a perilous one in the days of the big spring drives on the swollen waters of the Fox and Driggs Rivers which converged near Seney.

It was the duty of the men to keep the logs continually on the move to prevent jams and pileups which might delay or stop the drive. When despite their strenuous efforts the logs piled up in great masses, it fell to their lot to break up the jams. Dressed in heavy woolen clothes, feet shod with heavy calked boots, the driver would hop from one log to another with his peavey in hand to find the key log which held the jam. Using his peavey as a pry he would tug at the log to get it started down stream, then on to the next log.

When the key log was released the pent-up logs behind it and the icy water would roar down the stream at express train speed, while the men scattered in all directions for safety to escape death. Each spring several men lost their lives when they failed to reach the shore or the batteau or river boat which followed the drive.

In the event of a death on the drive there was no time to stop to give the body a decent burial. A few men were assigned to dig a trench on the river bank and lay their fellow worker in a grave unmarked except for his calked boots hung in a nearby tree—an unsung hero who lost his life that American homes might be built.

Frank N. Cookson was foreman on the drive for the Chicago Lumber Company on the Driggs River one spring when there was an unusually great head of water from the melting snow and the heavy rains. An old, experienced river-hog applied to him for a job. Cookson had a full crew but knew that some of the men would become disabled or would not be able to withstand the rigors of the drive to the end. He was skeptical, however, of the applicant because of his boasting.

"Why," claimed the man, "my working for you will insure that your crew will have no accidents. With me on the job, nothing can happen to your men. I'm the lucky ace in the deck."

Conditions were hazardous at best and another man would be needed, so the oldtimer was hired.

One day a large log jam began to form at a sharp bend in the river. Several of the most skilled rivermen set about trying to locate the key log causing the trouble, the oldtimer among them. As the log was finally loosened it shot down the river to be followed by hundreds of logs under the immense pressure of the icy water. The men bounded over the log jam to the safety of the river banks. The oldtimer jumped back to regain his footing on a large log he had stood on but it had joined the others in its mad rush down stream. Instead of landing on the log and to safety, he dropped into the boiling water and was sucked out of sight between the churning mass of pine.

Cookson and the men ran down the banks with their peavies and pikepoles poised, watching for the river-hog to bob up between the milling, bumping logs. Only

THE SPRING DRIVE

Millions of logs and pulpwood were driven down the rivers to the mills at spring flood time.

a miracle could save him now. If he came through alive, he would undoubtedly be badly injured.

As the men ran down the banks the old driver's red woolen cap came to the surface, bobbing up and down in the rushing water. Nothing was seen of its owner.

"Well, boys," said the foreman, "I guess he's a goner. Let's go down and find his body."

As they rounded a bend in the stream they came upon the old riverman standing waist deep in the surging water, shouting and waving his arms:—

"I'm all right. Didn't I tell you, Cookson, you would have no bad accidents if I was part of your crew!"

Cookson scratched his head.

"Now, that's what I call a miracle. There was so much water coming out from under that jam and through it by the pressure above that there must have been a swift undercurrent, so it caught that oldtimer and carried him ahead of the logs to that sand bar below."

The boys that evening at the way camp had a good laugh, but they all conceded that the old man was O.K. and the crew was lucky to have him as a member.

CHAPTER TWELVE

"Dad" O'Brien's Pigs

DAD" O'BRIEN raised pigs as a hobby and as a source
of food. They were of no particular breed—just pigs.
He fed them mostly with the garbage from "The O'Brien
House" and they were allowed to run wild, foraging for
the balance of their living, on acorns in the nearby woods
and the swill that was thrown out by the housewives in
the town. Others in the neighborhood had similar herds
of half-wild hogs, so that the community at certain times
of the year was over-run by pigs. Wherever one looked
there were dozens of black, black and white, white, red
and white, black, red and white hogs with their litters of
young, rooting, eating, lying in the mudholes, fighting
and socializing.

Whenever Dad needed pork for his hotel he would set
his butcher, a retired lumberjack, to catching and slaugh-
tering whatever pigs he could catch grazing about town,
regardless of their ownership. Whenever an argument
developed over whose pig was whose, Dad's Irish wit settled the dispute.

"Don't ye see me brand on the baste?"

The animal may not have had a brand but Dad would
invent one on the spot, pointing to some scar or mark
which happened to be on the hog. If no mark was present
he would call attention to some breed showing up on the

pig and declare that no one else ever owned a breed of that type and that it was his.

Other hog owners seldom seriously disputed Dad's ownership, for pigs were so plentiful that they had no difficulty in supplying all their needs for pork. Dad even salted his pork for the winter and sold the excess to the lumber camps.

Dad's "sowbelly" was a favorite in the lumber woods. It was "pass Dad's sowbelly," "pass Dad's grease" or "there's nothing like Dad's pork to eat with your morning-glories (pancakes)." Stacks upon stacks of rich, brown "morning-glories" were the jack's favorite breakfast, heaps of them saturated with bacon grease and covered with corn syrup. There was nothing like them to "stick to the ribs." It was claimed in nearby camps that the men would have starved to death if it were not for Dad's roaming herd of pigs.

The O'Brien House was operated on a very orderly basis, considering the conditions in the new pine country and in comparison to the manner in which the other hotels and saloons were conducted. The lobby, then called the lounging room, was occupied by the better class of trade, such as drummers, dudes from the city, superintendents, bosses and business men of the town and neighborhood. The common jacks were not allowed to enter this room unless they had private business with the proprietor. Off the bar and lobby was a large dining room equipped with long tables covered with oil cloth. Chairs were used instead of benches, such as were used in the lumberjack dining room.

Pork was the chief entree on the unwritten menu. The common expression of the waitress was:

A TYPICAL LUMBER TOWN BOARDING AND ROOMING HOUSE

The home of G. W. Earle, the lumber operator of Hermansville, stands on the hill.

"Tea or coffee? And how do you like your pork?"

P. K. Small, a boarder at Dad's when he could get enough money for an honest meal, once remarked:—

"Jees, don't Dad ever have any beef? Every time I eat here, it's pork, pork, pork. I know Dad could get some beef if the tight old bastard would loosen up. Don't he ever get tired of pork all the time, like us jacks do?"

Dad's ambition was to give his children an education. The couple had seven sons, four who survived infancy, and all of them were raised on pork from the beginning. Their father was instrumental in establishing the first elementary school in Seney and saw to it that his sons attended without delinquency. Pork from Dad's roving herd helped send William, the eldest, through high school and law school, after which the young man became the prosecuting attorney in Alger county. Frank lost his life in a hunting accident. Ed, the third boy, got his start via the pork barrel and also became an attorney and followed William as prosecuting attorney in Alger county.

Steve, the seventh son, was directed to medicine by his ambitious mother. As soon as he graduated from the Seney school he was packed off to medical college, no doubt with a pork sandwich in his coat pocket. He opened practise at Munising after graduation and later became attached to a large medical clinic in Chicago where he passed away while still a young man, due, some said, to overwork in his new position.

The first summer after William returned home from college, Bellaire asked "Dad" what he thought of his son's college education. "Dad" screwed up his Irish face and replied:—

"I'm dissypointed. That kid's been at college for nine

months and I kin still understand every word he says."

As "Dad's" boys were getting places in their selected fields, business at Seney was beginning to drop off. The pine was almost all cut. The oldtime lumberjacks were disappearing from the scene. The old, roistering town became too quiet for "Dad" O'Brien. With their boys gone and the pressing financial needs of the family past, he and Ma decided to move to Grand Marais, pigs and all. But by that time, Grand Marais, once a rough lumber town, had become respectable. Pigs were ruled off the streets. "Dad" was unhappy. So were his pigs, now confined in pens. Another lumber town tradition had gone the way of civilization.

CHAPTER THIRTEEN

Stalled in the Snowdrift

ONE WINTER a fierce northwest blizzard started on Monday morning and continued through Thursday, the worst storm in years. The Manistique Logging Railroad's mixed train left Grand Marais on Monday morning for Seney to connect with the D.S.S.&A. train. The passengers consisted of a number of commercial traveling men, one woman, the daughter of Saulson, a Grand Marais dry goods merchant, lumberjacks and a few others, a total of forty people including the train crew. At Camp Seven hill the train stalled in a deep drift.

A member of the crew waded through hip-deep snow to the nearest telephone box and called Grand Marais station for help. Another engine and snowplow were dispatched as soon as the emergency crew could be gathered. The relief train raced to the scene with snow flying like plumes on both sides of the track. The snow plow and both engines drove the train for three miles, puffing and snorting through the drifts which were getting higher and higher. Then they stalled between a high fence which the railroad had built to keep snow from drifting onto the track. As the head engine struck the drift, snow rolled down its smokestack and dampened the fires under the boiler.

At a signal from the engineer of the head engine, the

train was reversed and backed down near the east branch of the Fox River. Here the fires were banked. The coal supply in the tenders was running low. It was decided to wait until morning and daylight, with the hope that the storm would subside.

There was no place for the passengers to sleep except on the seats. The coach was kept warm by the steam from the forward engine. The passengers made the young woman as comfortable as possible, offering her mackinaws and mittens. But sleep was out of the question. The men passed the long, black night playing cards by the lights of dim kerosene lamps overhead, told stories and entertained themselves until daylight.

When morning and a faint glow of light appeared the storm was raging with greater fierceness than the night before. The wind had increased and blew the light snow over the train and covered some of the cars. The high board fence on the west side of the track was completely blanketed. The snow was twelve feet deep in the windrows.

It was impossible to see far in any direction for the whirling blizzard. There was nothing on the train to eat. There was plenty of clear, fresh water flowing under the railroad bridge. By noon the passengers began to feel the pangs of hunger. A search was made for some means of getting over the deep drifts to Seney for food. A pair of snowshoes was found on one of the engine tenders. Lon Myers, a powerful brakesman and experienced woodsman, volunteered to make the attempt. The snow was light and fluffy. When he stood on the snowshoes he sank to his knees. As he set out the light snow rose in clouds over his head. He was out of sight within a few feet from the train.

He reached the village late that afternoon in an extremely exhausted condition. There he borrowed Jim Drysdale's team of sleigh dogs and tobaggon which the owner used in traveling to the different camps when the roads were clogged, delivering shoes to the employees.

Myers had the Andrew Daly family, who operated a boarding house, cook and prepare enough food to fill a large clothes basket and two large jugs of coffee. He rested while the food was being cooked and packed, then started back to the marooned train and its hungry, snowbound occupants, his huskies barking and floundering in the deep drifts. It was late that night when he reached the stalled train. Food never tasted so good to the anxious passengers and crew.

On Wednesday and Thursday Myers made trips to Seney with the dogteam for food. It was impossible to make any progress with the deeply buried train. The low temperature froze the snow packed by the engine. The rails were glared with ice, so that the driving wheels of the locomotive merely spun without moving forward. The train crew advised that it would be best for everyone to stay near the river where there was water to drink and to keep the engine boilers filled.

The storm ended Thursday night. Then the work began. The wisest method to make progress was to run the forward engine ahead toward Seney. The engineers drove ahead as far as they dared, taking care that the wheels did not leave the track. Then they pulled back and set all hands, crew and passengers to shovel off the packed snow. Fortunately, there were several snow and coal shovels on the train. About noon on Friday the train ran out of coal. The train crew kept the fires burning in both engines by cutting and dragging dead tamarack wood over the deep snow. Gradually, laborously, the train was worked back to Seney late Friday night, the occupants having been held prisoners for five days.

Saturday morning one of the larger engines was sent ahead with the snowplow while the other locomotive followed with the passengers and freight, plus a week's accumulation of mail, and reached Manistique just as darkness had settled over that mill town.

CHAPTER FOURTEEN

A Hot Election in Seney

ELECTIONS were exciting events in Seney. Strong drinks flowed freely. Candidates made the rounds of the saloons to buy liquor for the boys gathered there. Some of the most inveterate imbibers followed them from tavern to tavern to be on hand for all the easy treats. Winning candidates were required to make the rounds again to help the boys celebrate their victories.

Lumberjacks came into town by the score, congregating in the twenty or more drinking places and holding heated discussions on the merits of their candidates and the election proposals. If reform candidates were in the running proposing to reform the moral life of the village or to tax the lumber companies more heavily, the lumber companies would release their men from work the day before election with instructions to vote properly if they wanted to keep the camps operating.

The voting, drinking and celebrating usually lasted into the "wee sma' hours" of the day after. Drunken brawls in which their sharp-shod boots stomped each other's faces accompanied the election excitement. Rival crews staged mob fights for the sheer joy of the battle of fists, boots and teeth. Seney elections were eagerly awaited by the burly citizens for the thrills they were certain to provide. They were also feared by the permanent residents of the town because of some of the horrible events which ensued.

One spring certain of the township officials decided to have a dry election. The county sheriff and the prosecuting attorney came to Seney and advised the saloon operators to close throughout Sunday and Monday, the day of election. Some of them had a hard time finding the keys to their front doors. They had not locked their establishments for such a long time that they had forgotten where they had hid the keys.

The sheriff made the rounds to make certain that the orders had been complied with. Seney was really dry for the first time in its riotous history, except for the quantities of liquor which had been bought on Saturday, hastily removed and hidden in barns, rooming houses and in the drinkers' pockets.

The lumberjacks were in a sorry plight. They had been drinking for several days and to be deprived of liquor so suddenly and on election day was something their systems could not stand. The amount of liquor they had concealed immediately after the closing order came was hardly enough for Sunday, much less for Monday, the big day. Only water from the town pump was available. Of this their thirsty throats partook freely but distastefully.

Tom Millen, the woods foreman from the Manistique Lumber Company, walked down the street to the front of Hugh Logan's saloon. Here he was waylaid by a gang of thirsty men who appealed to him for assistance in their dire distress. Tom had no authority to set aside the ruling but his big heart went out to the sufferers. In exasperation he shouted to Logan, who was standing at the window of his locked saloon:

"Holy old Mackinaw, Hughy, throw open them doors and give them boys a drink. If you don't, they'll drink up the Fox River and spoil the drive."

At this spring election Jim Harcourt and Wesley Sparling were candidates for the office of township clerk. Harcourt worked in the woods and on the log drives and was a great favorite with the men. Sparling was in charge of the Hall and Buell lumber operations and was also well liked. The voters were out in full force.

Bellaire, working as a clerk in the Morse & Schneider general store, was one of the best educated men in the village. Harcourt asked Bellaire's employers if they would release him from his work for the day to serve on the election board, which they did. Bellaire agreed to serve if he was not required to "do any crooked work."

Many of the voters could neither read or write and had to be instructed where to place the "X." Bellaire was to be one of the instructors. He had his instructions too. He was to watch how each man voted. If he voted for the "right" man, he was to wink his right eye. If the voter chose the "wrong" man, he was to wink his left eye.

The men from the woods and the voters of the township were loyal to their friends. During the day when the first man voted for the "wrong" man, Bellaire winked his left eye and waited to see what would happen. He noticed one of Harcourt's supporters move to the door. Bellaire excused himself and slipped through the back door. As he approached the front of the polling place, the "wrong" voter was coming out. A hand shot out and caught him at the butt of his right ear. The man bounded into the air so swiftly that a kick, intended to help him along, missed its mark.

The election was contested hard all day long. Great excitement prevailed. Both parties had their challengers. Many were required to swear in their votes. As soon as the polls closed, the counting of the ballots began.

The polling place was jammed with fifty men. Bellaire called out the names on each ticket for the two clerks to tally. There was a murmur or a shout as each name was read. The suspense was great. When more than half the ballots had been counted, Bellaire announced that even if all the uncounted ballots were for Sparling, Harcourt would be elected.

Both Harcourt and Sparling stood behind Bellaire and advised him to make the count accurate. Upon the completion of the count, Bellaire declared the result. Harcourt shouted to the crowd that he was the winner and the new township clerk. The men yelled at the top of their lungs for their favorite.

The men outside, numbering over a hundred, wanted to see and hear what all the shouting and cheering was about. The doors were crowded from the inside and could not be opened. The outsiders formed a battering ram and crashed through the door, forcing those inside through the two-by-four railing dividing the gallery from the tellers. As the railing gave way, someone grabbed a two-by-four and swung it over the heads of the inrushing men.

The wood stove was overturned, spilling burning coals onto the plank floor, setting it on fire. The election board, thinking that the intruders were attempting to raid the ballot box, gathered it up and ducked out the back door to safety. Billy Ganner, a lumberjack, had pinned Ross

Sweet, one of the challengers, up against the wall and cocked his right fist to deal him a crushing blow on his face. Before the blow had time to land, Harcourt threw himself between the men and upset them onto the floor. That stopped the carnage.

Enthusiastic friends boosted Harcourt upon their shoulders and started a march down the street, yelling for their man.

The election board returned to the building which looked as though it had been struck by a tornado. They ran over to Andrew Daly's saloon, brought back several pails of water and extinguished the fire which by that time had gotten a good start. They opened the windows to clear out the smoke and braced the door shut with a two-by-four. They pried up the stove, placed two-by-fours under it and threw it out the back door.

The night was cold and the temperature in the election place was near zero. It was midnight before the tellers finished their tallying and made out their election report.

As they were clearing away the wreckage they heard a noise coming out from under a smashed steel voting booth. There they found "Professor" J. A. Chisholm, the school principal of Seney, still hiding.

"Is the fight over?" he asked in a shaking voice.

He had dived into a booth when the mad rush came. The booth had collapsed and pinned him inside the walls. Aside from a bad fright, he was uninjured. He later became accustomed to the rough play of the lumberjacks and became the school commissioner of Schoolcraft county.

One spring Tom McCann, a powerfully built Irish bartender in Phil Grondin's saloon, was a candidate for township supervisor. The saloon was a favorite hangout for the natives and jacks and Tom was well liked. He had been a deputy sheriff in the township for several years. It was a common saying that he always got his man and the only way a fugitive could get away from him was to "take the road with him." He was easily nominated.

Wesley Sparling was being boosted for the same office on the opposition ticket. The two men put up a stiff campaign, with treating and promising, so the excitement ran in high gear. Dr. Bohn was chairman of the election board. C. E. Morse was clerk and Billy Marks and Bellaire were the tellers.

The McCann men had hundreds of typewritten slips made and given to the lumberjacks and others with instructions to vote, then return to the saloon for free drinks. McCann was presiding at the bar and was offering free drinks for votes.

The voting began. The jacks crowded in early in order to be in on as many of the treats as possible. Bellaire soon saw them voting ballots by the handfuls. He called this to the attention of the chairman, whose advice was to let them vote as they pleased. When the first large crowd of jacks had voted and left for Grondin's, Dr. Bohn instructed Bellaire to catch the hand of the next man trying to place more than one ballot in the box. Soon a big fellow came up. He was staggering and clutched a handful of ballots in his big fist. Bellaire caught his hand and pulled the slips from his fingers. The voter struck Bellaire over the head with his free hand and almost knocked him from his chair. The teller hung onto him and soon had ample assistance. They forced the hand open and a dozen slips fell to the floor.

A motion was made and carried to declare the whole election illegal. The voted slips were promptly thrown into the stove. The supporters of each candidate rushed out to rally enough men to carry the election on, but most of the men were by this time too interested in free drinks to leave the saloons.

The crowd present was instructed to vote again. A table was placed so that only one man could pass through an aisle and place his vote face down on a table. Bellaire then placed the paper in the ballot box.

McCann won the election by a scant majority. Both sides took the result with the best of grace. Both sides gathered at Grondin's tavern and stood treat in turn. It was a successful election and a good time was had by all.

CHAPTER FIFTEEN

The Lumberjack Fight of the Ages

No more picturesque early Michigan pioneer lived than the resourceful, self-reliant old-time lumberjack. These powerful men stood out apart and distinct from all other early characters in the Wolverine state—the conquerors of the vast wilderness of pine which stretched from Lake Michigan and from the Straits of Mackinaw to Lake Superior.

Virgin trees towering from one hundred to one hundred and fifty feet high, with lower limbs forty feet from the ground; many human generations old, bowed at the coming of the men from the pine lands of Maine, from the Scandinavian countries and from the Saginaw Valley and the Cadillac country of Michigan. Before them the wilderness melted within a period of twenty years, only to become a tangle of brush and burned-over jungle when the carnage was completed.

The Eskimo was a weakling compared to these men of iron muscle and indominitable will who thrived in the intense cold and only laughed the louder when the mercury dropped out of the bottom of the thermometer.

Throughout the long, cold, desolate winter months these hardy men felled the tall, straight pine which measured from four to eight feet in diameter, cut them into log lengths and hauled them in mammoth loads to the rollways on the river banks. When the warm spring sun melted the deep snow and flooded the rivers to their banks, these same men rode the logs down the angry waters to the outside world and the mills which processed them into lumber for the building of our cities and industrial plants. They defied the bitter cold and the blinding storms of winter and the rain and freeze of spring to supply the demand for timber.

It was a common event of their toil to struggle at their work in the face of destruction beneath the grinding menace of a log jam where a small error of judgment could bring tons upon tons of mighty timbers down upon them to crush their bodies into pulp and to be buried beside the rivers they loved.

Theirs is a story of long, bitter fights against the icy weather, blinding snow and torrential floods, a story which is part of the saga of early America. Their reign was short, lasting but a little over half a century. This unique species presented a unique race which it would be difficult to match in any other walk of life. They lived in an age when men were close to nature and drew from her dispositions, which were both kindly and cruel, beneficient and vengeful.

Relieved of the strenuousness of their occupation at the end of the cutting and driving season, they turned all the forces of their wonderful energies which carried them far when other men halted, to channels in which a gentle current made flood enough. Instead of average pleasures, they sought orgies to give them recreation. They ran to wild excesses of drinking, fighting and "loving." Yet those who knew them could only admire their picturesque figures of such tremendous energies running riot.

The old-time lumberjack of the north was a splendid specimen of physical manhood. Drunk or sober, short or tall, he carried his steel-muscled body like a king. He would fight at the drop of a hat and fight to the bitter end. He had his code. Rough in speech, dress and manner, loving life, loving crudely, still he was a gentle man through it all. No man could offend, insult or molest a woman on the street or even speak lightly of a woman of good reputation without suffering swift and violent justice at the hands of his fellow lumberjacks.

Hand-to-hand conflicts, many of them over trivial matters, and some with no logical excuse whatever, took place with great frequency, and many of them, unless stopped, ended disastrously, the loser being fortunate to escape with his life. Broken bones were a mere detail—the participants "going to it" with no quarter asked or given. To be sure, there were bullies, men who picked fights at every opportunity and who became notorious and later legendary throughout the camps because of their great physical prowess, hated for their cowardly attacks on weaker men.

There were those who would take on all comers in the woods, on the street or in saloons and fought because they loved fighting. In the latter class were found fighters who would take the part of weaker men who usually were the objects of the bullies' attention when seeking a battle.

One such lumberjack was Tim Kaine, a prominent and outstanding character in the old Seney days. Volumes could be written about this two-fisted man who rose from a stripling to the envied position of lumber camp foreman.

In those days, being a foreman of a camp of a hundred or more men meant of necessity that he was able to whip any man in the camp if required to mete out justice or to subdue a trouble maker. From the stories which still float about Seney Tim Kaine was the man who could do just that. Possibly hundreds of battles were chalked up to his credit, most of them in the defence of weaker individuals and the victims of bullying. His characteristic for fairness and desire for justice led to his death in the defence of a boy lumberjack who was being roughly treated by a camp bully.

Kaine's strength was prodigious. His admirers stated that he never picked a fight except for a just cause and that he was never bested in a fair battle.

The battle which remains a classic in the memories of the oldtimers was the result of an incident which happened when Kaine was driving a team of horses in John Dugan's lumber camp. Dugan was known as a slave driver. It was a byword among his men that no one saw the camp in the light of day except Sundays. He drove his men out of camp long before dawn and kept them at their work in the woods until they could not see the trees and could chop no more.

Kaine was not feeling well one day and planned to take a few days' leave from camp and rest up at a rooming house in Seney. One of the young men in the bunk next to his was also ailing from a serious cold which kept him coughing throughout the night. Kaine planned to take the youngster with him and bring him back to the camp after he had recovered. He explained the situation to Dugan and asked for his pay slip and a few days off for both men.

Dugan retorted:—

"You damned slackers! I'll make you a whole lot sicker!"

Raising the big hardwood canthook he was leaning on he struck down Kaine in his tracks without warning and before Kaine could defend himself. When Kaine regained consciousness he realized that if he made any attempt to get even then it would mean an unmerciful beating at the hands of the slave-driving boss.

Tim went to the camp office, drew his time slip, packed his belongings in his "turkey" and left on foot, vowing to the camp clerk and his chums in the camp that he would get even with Dugan for his inhuman treatment if it took him the rest of his life.

His opportunity did not come for five years. The lumber company discharged Dugan that spring for his treatment of the men under him. Kaine never forgot the blow from the canthook handle. He kept preparing himself for that day when he would meet his cruel antagonist on fair ground. He worked hard in the woods and on the spring drives. He drank less and ate well. He practised boxing with the men in the bunkhouse and wrestled in friendly matches with the crew. He was getting ready.

At the end of his five year wait his chance came. As he, Ed Cookson, Jerry Holland and other lumberjacks were standing on the depot platform as the train pulled into Seney, Holland spied Dugan alight from the train and start across the street to the hotel. Nudging Kaine, Holland whispered:·

"There's the man you've been waiting for, Tim."

Kaine, his eyes lighting up with the rage he had supressed for five long years, stepped up to Dugan, who was dressed in "city clothes" and asked if he was Dugan, his boss in the lumber camp.

"No," Dugan replied, his face blanching as he recognized he was in for a battle without a canthook in his hands.

"You're a God damned liar," shouted Tim. "I'll give you just half a minute to get that coat off for the beating of your life."

Though fights were a common occurrence at almost any hour of the day or night on the streets of Seney, the crowd which poured out from the saloons and homes of the town, sensed that a real battle between two noted fighters was about to take place. They surged around the pair as they prepared for the set-to. Some of the onlookers climbed upon box cars to get a bird's-eye view of the proceedings.

Tim let fly a fist which connected with Dugan's head and received a vicious poke which would have felled an ordinary man. The fight was on in all its viciousness. Standing toe to toe, the battlers' fists flew like four axes in a log chopping contest and with just as much force. Steel-hard muscles drove rock-hard fists to face and body. Kaine connected with a pile-driving punch to Dugan's eye, closing it. Blood streamed from Dugan's face. Battering-ram blows sounded like hammer blows on an oxen's head. The men seemed evenly matched.

It was a continuous round and a slugging match with no rests. Both men were putting every ounce of their brute force into their blows, their arms as tough as the trees they felled.

The battlers broke away from time to time, to circle, dodge and strike again. Bystanders who crowded in too close were knocked down unceremoniously as the men lunged at each other. At each lunge Kaine and Dugan came together like two bull moose. Kaine seemed to be in perfect physical condition from his long training and abstinence from liquor. He forced his opponent back into the circling crowd and brought him to his knees with a vicious jab to the jaw. Someone pushed Dugan up and back into the ring. The push sent him to Kaine who slugged him back again.

Dugan's nose was now streaming red, his clothes were torn to ribbons and he was weakening slightly. His blows were beginning to miss their mark. His roars became grunts of pain. He was knocked down and into the crowd repeatedly, only to rally with the reserve strength every lumberman possessed for emergencies. Fear now glistened in his bloodshot eye. Perhaps memories of previous rough and tumble battles in which hob-nailed boots played an important part rose in his mind as he desperately fought back.

Dugan came up from the dust of the street time and time again, almost forcing the vengeful Kaine to the ground with his mad lunges. Tim took a lot of punishment and bit the dusty road more than once. There were times when it looked as though Dugan might land the deciding blow when Kaine was rocked back on his heels. But Tim had waited for this moment and though he fell more than once under the hammering fists of the woods boss, he protected himself with flailing feet until he could get back on his feet again.

The fight went on for over an hour, although no one thought of time. The crowd of Kaine partisans went wild. They yelled themselves hoarse. Finally and gradually

Kaine's superior strength, backed by a rage of five years, **counted.** A well-aimed blow lifted Dugan off his feet and flattened him on the ground, blood bursting from his nose and mouth, his clothes torn to shreds.

Though weakened, Dugan got on his feet again. He kept on the defensive, dodging as he could the lethal fists of the avenger. Tim, seeing that his opponent was weakening, kept up his merciless attack and drove in smash after smash until Dugan was practically helpless. With his head down he swayed on his feet, but his bulldog tenacity kept his fists pounding feebly. The crowd was in a frenzy. Dugan, the despised Lagree of the lumber camps, was going down to defeat at the hands of his early victim.

The onlookers crowded in for the finish which was due in any moment. Kaine let fly a terrific uppercut which connected with Dugan's sagging jaw. The blow flung him back into the crowd, with Kaine following after him, ready to deal another, his fists cocked and his tired eyes still blazing.

Here the fight might have ended in the death of Dugan who was now helpless to protect himself against Tim's ferocious battering. Ethics of the woods now permitted Kaine to finish his opponent with his boots and to kick him into insensibility. But his friend, Jerry Holland, stepped in and caught Kaine's arm. "That's enough, Tim," he counseled, as he drew the victor away from the battered Dugan. "You've got your revenge and plenty of it. Let him alone now or you'll have a killing on your conscience."

"All right, Jerry," panted Kaine, then slowly, without looking at the beaten man, he turned away, wiped the blood and sweat off his face with his tattered shirt sleeve, picked up his coat and walked up the main street of Seney with a hundred men and boys yelling at his heels.

Dugan struggled to his feet a few minutes later and, supported by one of the men, reeled toward the hotel, a man beaten in body and spirit.

Today in Seney and its environs old, toothless veterans of the woods will tell you of this battle of the ages.

"Yesiree, I was right there," they will avow, their eyes blazing and the fists gesticulating in the imitation of the hero Kaine. "Yesiree, that there man Kaine was a lulu! I never seed such a battle. You know, I was jest a kid then. But I shook Tim's hand after that fight. I'll never forget it."

CHAPTER SIXTEEN

The Murder of Tim Kaine

VIOLENT DEATH was not an unusual occurrence in and about Seney. There are many tales of men done to death during those riotous days in the "80ties and '90ties, men secretly disposed of by gamblers to cover up their cheating, by highwaymen, who waylaid lumberjacks for their winter's stake, and by saloon keepers and bartenders who "rolled" the men down from the woods in order to conceal their robberies.

A number of hot-blooded murders were committed in the saloons and the streets of Seney by men seeking revenge for some previous wrong or grievance, fancied or real. Several deaths came about through the battles lumberjacks and others engaged in while under the influence of hard drink. Fatal accidents in the camps were expected every winter and drownings and death were frequent on the dangerous spring drives.

The murder of Tim Kaine, the popular foreman in one of the Manistique Lumber Company's logging camps, was one of the most sensational in the brief but turbulent history of Seney.

The camps had been having considerable trouble with the men in their crews. Wages were low that winter. The snow was waist deep. The grub was poor. The men were paid from $20.00 to $25.00 a month plus board and a straw-covered bunk to sleep in. The market for logs was at a low ebb and the lumber camp operators were pushing the bosses to get out more timber than usual. This in turn made the bosses surly and they drove their men all the harder. Men began to leave one camp for another to seek better conditions. This migration broke up the camp crews and slowed the logging operations. One thing aggravated another.

In order to stop the quitting and traveling from camp to camp, the company for which Tim Kaine worked ruled that if a man started to work in the camps and remained until the cut was finished or until the spring breakup, he would be paid his wages in full. If he quit one of the camps and attempted to draw his wages, the camp clerks were directed to deduct two dollars a month as a penalty. This practise made for even more discontent and led to many fights and lawsuits.

Tim Kaine was foreman in the camp in which Isaac Stecher was an axeman. The day before Christmas Stecher appeared at the camp office and requested his wages to date. Kaine told the camp clerk, Avery Thrall, that he would have to carry out the company rule and deduct the two dollars a month from Stecher's pay. Stecher protested and demanded that he receive everything he had coming for his work, but the clerk gave him his time slip with the deduction. In rage Stecher left the camp with his only possessions stuffed in his "turkey", vowing he would get even with the foreman.

Kaine and several of the men from the nearby camps spent their Christmas holiday in Seney. Most of the men stayed with their families for a bit of celebrating and friendly drinking. Stecher and Kaine were seen eating

EARLY FALL CUTTINGS

Horses and oxen were used to skid logs to piles from which big sleighs hauled them to the rollways after freeze-up.

U. of Mich. School of Natural Resources.

at the same table in the Globe Hotel and they seemed to be on most friendly terms.

The night of Christmas Eve was unusually dark. There was a threat of a snow storm in the atmosphere and the clouds hung low over the little town. There was a great deal of sickness among the children of Seney and the good people of Seney decided to dispense with the usual public Christmas tree and entertainment in the town hall. Such gatherings would only spread the illness to others. Some of the village women had visited the nearby camps and the local business places to raise a bit of money, almost one hundred dollars, to buy the kids a treat in their own homes. The money was turned over to a committee which bought and made neat packages of small gifts, candies and mixed nuts for each family where there were children.

John Bellaire was appointed Santa Claus. He donned a great goatskin coat and a Santa Claus mask. John Van Alstein, the railroad telegrapher, drove the team of horses and sleigh loaded down with the treats. The men tied bells on the horses' harness and drove around to each dwelling where children lived. Bellaire carried the packages into the homes, passed them out and dealt out handfuls of loose candy and nuts from his big overcoat pockets.

As the men stopped their horses before the Hugh Logan residence they heard shouting in Logan's saloon on the opposite side of the street. From the sound of things they knew there was trouble brewing.

Bellaire removed his mask and the men waited. Logan burst open the saloon door and shoved Stecher out into the snow-covered street, telling him not to start trouble in his place.

Tim Kaine came through the door into the street as if

he were looking for someone. A crowd came out of the saloon and followed closely behind Kaine, urging him to get that "SOB" who tried to start a fight on Christmas Eve. Kaine walked cautiously down the snow-packed sidewalk. As he passed an alley between the saloon and a restaurant Stecher lunged at him, striking him twice with a long knife. Kaine slumped back and fell into the arms of the men behind him. They carried him into the saloon and laid him on the floor. Logan called for someone to get Dr. Bohn whose office was in the Fell building across the street. Upon examining the man, the doctor pronounced him dead.

The crowd of men turned to Stecher who stood fixed on the sidewalk with a long open jackknife still in his right hand.

"I didn't want to kill him", he blubbered. "I just wanted to cripple him."

Someone called for a rope and talk of lynching was shouted about.

Bellaire ran to Phil Grondin's saloon to get Deputy Sheriff Tom McCann. McCann took Stecher to the village jail and appointed two men to watch over him until morning. Kaine's body was removed to the local undertaking establishment and the men who had witnessed the cold-blooded murder went back to celebrating in the saloons.

Stecher was taken under heavy guard to the county jail at Manistique the next morning to await trial at the January term of Circuit Court. He pleaded not guilty and claimed that Kaine had cheated him of part of his winter's wages. The judge sentenced him to seven and a half years in Marquette prison.

Bellaire, at the time, acted as a special correspondent for the Detroit Evening News. He had witnessed the murder and knew of the quarrel which had led to the killing. He and Van Alstein went to the railroad station and wired the News in code a complete description of the affair and the incidents which led up to it. Almost immediately a coded reply came back requesting Bellaire to wire complete particulars and spare no expense. Here was a "hot" story from Seney which corroborated the wild tales about the wide open hell-town of the north. As fast as Van Alstein could tick off the message Bellaire wrote the story, sparing no detail and no expense. The next day the News carried a full account of the killing of Tim Kaine.

The Associated Press Dispatches sent the news broadcast. Kaine's brother, who was a reporter on the "Toronto Globe" of Toronto, Canada, caught the message as it came over the wire to his newspaper. He wired Bellaire at Seney and came to take the body of his brother to his old home for burial.

CHAPTER SEVENTEEN

"Silver Jack" Driscoll

THE MICHIGAN lumber camps never produced a more unique or fabulous character, or one who was more maligned, than "Silver Jack" Driscoll. The woods of Maine had its fabled Paul Bunyan but the true Bull-o'-the-Woods" of Michigan in fact and deed was the prematurely white-haired Driscoll.

Born in Peterboro, Ontario, he was among those thousands of Canadian youths who left their homes when the tales and glamour of the harvesting of Michigan's white pine cast its spell upon rugged, two-fisted men seeking fortune and excitement in other parts.

A plume of white hair against his jet-black locks gave him his nickname which stuck to him until his death of pneumonia in a L'Anse rooming house at the age of sixty-five.

Even at the age of eighteen when he hit the roaring lumber and mill town of Saginaw, Jack was a dashing figure, six-feet-four in his stocking feet, a rugged, lovable man, a friend of the weak, generous to his last penny, with great attraction to women.

As a skilled woodsman with an ax and a fearless riverman, the young Irish-Canadian soon became the envy of all who knew him. Forced into a fight in one of the camps when he defended a younger jack from a woods bully, he gained a reputation for fighting which followed him to the grave.

It was after the time John L. Sullivan was making a tour of the lumber camp towns where he challenged all comers to fight him in the ring. It was at one of these affairs in a town "opera house," that Tom Conrad, a powerful bully, answered the challenge. Conrad was in the balcony and in hurrying to the ring, he fell and broke his leg. It was this same Conrad, who in later years, bullied the boy in the lumber camp, where Silver Jack was employed. Conrad continually picked on the youth and made his camp life a torture. None of the jacks dared to interfere for fear of a beating at the hands of the bully. During one particular bad day, Driscoll ordered the fellow to lay off the boy or take the consequences. The fight was on but of short duration. Conrad swung with his right. Driscoll ducked and landed a sledge-hammer blow on his jaw. Conrad fell like an ox struck by a poleaxe. Silver Jack's reputation as a fighter was made.

His first really serious encounter took place in the Ontario House at Pruddenville with a fighter of wide repute. "Frenchy" Fournier, one of the most powerful men in the Saginaw Valley, had heard of Jack's prowess in the camps and sought a fight. He, too, was a bully and would attack any man just for the pleasure of beating him helpless.

Fournier found Jack in a saloon in Pruddenville and tried to provoke him into a fight. Jack avoided him. Jack was courting a girl. "Frenchy" learned of this and insulted her on the street, knowing that she would report it to her friend. That evening while Jack was standing at the bar in the Ontario House, "Frenchy" entered and banged his big fist on the bar.

"This is the damnedest fist in the Saginaw Valley," he declared, looking Jack in the eye.

Jack stepped into the middle of the sawdust covered floor, threw off his mackinaw and said:

"Well, we might as well decide that right now."

The bully swung a ham-sized fist at Jack's face. Like a cat the young woodsman dodged and came up with a haymaker which caught his antagonist flush on the jaw. Fournier dropped limp to the floor and lay there. "Silver Jack" looked at the prostrate man in surprise, then casually called the onlookers to the bar for a drink.

Word of Jack's fighting ability spread by way of the lumberjack telegraph. Wherever he appeared he was followed by awed men and boys who hung on his word and hoped that a challenger might appear to engage their hero. This fame gave him a swagger. Thereafter he never avoided a fight, though he never deliberately sought one.

His delight was to barge into a dance and steal another fellow's girl, which usually resulted in fisticuffs. Unlike others who later adopted the name of "Silver Jack," he was never found in the company of women of ill-repute. One lumberjack, who had taken the name to give himself an undeserved reputation as a fighter, worked for Frank Cookson in the camps. He was known as a bad number, a gambler and crook, who toted two pistols and wore a broad red sash around his neck. He was caught cheating at cards in a Ewen gambling room and was shot. His escapades helped to blacken the character of the original "Silver Jack," about whom exaggerated tales soon sprang up, making him a marked man, who was feared and loved in turn.

"Silver Jack" turned up in many places at various times. Wherever he appeared, it seemed that someone would challenge him. At the little town of Evart a stranger strode into a barroom and in a loud voice asked if "Silver Jack" was there. Jack stepped into the middle of the floor and met him.

"I'm Angus Bronson," announced the newcomer. "I'm the toughest man on the whole Tittabawassee River. I hear that you're the best man in these parts, so I come all the way up here to see if that is so."

Jack replied in a quiet tone:

"You may be the best man down your way. I'm not looking for trouble, but since you made that long trip just to find out, I'll have to accomodate you."

Immediately the hangers-on made a circle about the men. Bronson looked around and asked whether there was anyone in the house who would see that he got a square deal. Several men stepped forward but Jack waved them back with his hand.

"Up in this country we fight fair."

The men squared off. They circled and jabbed, eyeing each other, waiting for an opening. Jack feinted. Bronson struck him a hard blow on the shoulder. Both men weighed over 190 pounds and were agile as toe dancers on the feet. Their heavy breathing was the only sound in the room except the smack of fists. Heavy, stone-like knuckles found flesh and bone hard to dent.

Half an hour passed with neither seeming to have the advantage. Then Jack landed a hard right to the jaw. Bronson's head jerked back. Jack bore in, pouring rights and lefts with crushing, brutish power. Another right to the jaw and Bronson went limp, his arms dropping to his sides. Jack stood and waited.

"I've had enough," breathed Bronson.

Silver Jack took his opponent by the arm and led him to the bar and called for the drinks for the house. Standing side by side the two battlers drank their fill, then staggered down the street, arm in arm, singing an old camp chanty.

Jack's hell-roaring got him into trouble in Saginaw. He had given the law considerable concern for his fighting and drinking. When he returned for a visit with his cronies, he was arrested for strong-arming a drunk on Franklin street and robbing him of $2.50. His friends claimed that it was a "put-up job" to get rid of him and railroad him out of town. Arrested with him was John Kelly, arraigned on the same charge. While the men were lodged in the Saginaw jail they set fire to their cell floor, hoping to escape in the confusion. The police smelled the smoke and came too early and their plot failed.

Silver Jack was tried and sentenced to a term of five years in Southern Michigan Prison at Jackson. Kelly was given a seven year term. The Saginaw officials expected to arrest them after their release to answer for their crime of incendiarism. Neither man returned there. While in prison "Silver Jack" was left in a cell with three other convicts. A quarrel started between him and his cell mates. The warden stated that he would have "laid them all out" had not one of the men pulled a knife and stabbed him, inflicting fifteen gashes in Jack's body. The prison surgeon said that the wounds were of such a nature that they would have killed any other man but Jack.

Jack was imbittered by his prison term. He was an unruly prisoner. At one time he almost escaped. Two cronies who worked in the prison shoe department with him nailed him up in a large wooden shoe packing box. The box was hauled on a dray with several other boxes before the guards missed him. They found one box heavier than the others which led to his apprehension. At the end of his time he came out with a poor discharge report.

After his release, he headed for Saginaw by train. Officers of the law met him at the station and ordered him to get back on the train and keep going, never to show his face in Saginaw. Weak from his long interment, he did not have the will to defy them. He knew that this was a ruse to save the officers' faces and to avoid revenge on the part of the fighter.

Once again Jack sought the place he loved best, the lumber camps in the north. Here, pale and soft-muscled, he gradually got himself into condition. The work was grueling and the hours long, but the food was ample and wholesome. By the end of the cutting and hauling season, he was in prime condition and hired out for the spring drive.

Two rival companies were fighting to get their logs down the river at the same time. The boss of the opposing drive was a bully who terrorized the rival company's men so that he had little difficulty in monopolizing the river at high water. Jack's company was worried and threatened with great financial loss if their logs were hung up after the floodwaters had subsided. Hearing of Jack's fighting ability and his willingness to solve any problem with his bare fists and boot calks, his boss sent for him and put him in charge of the drive. He promptly sent his toughest men down the river and had them control the dams and keep the logs going. The rival logs were shunted into a boom in slack water. When the bully boss found his way blocked by Jack's men, he appeared at the head of the drive and demanded that Jack hold up his logs and let his own timber pass the boom. The result was inevitable. Jack was there for one purpose and one only. The men promptly clashed. Jack came off with two missing front teeth but succeeded in biting off one of his opponent's ears. The fight was declared a draw but Jack's logs reached the mill first.

Dan Dunn, a saloon keeper and "hoodlum" operator, whole law-breaking had driven him from Roscommon to Seney, opened equally notorious joints in the latter place. He was having trouble with the Harcourt brothers, Tom, Luke, Jim, Dick, Bill and Steve. The Harcourts operated a saloon and the White House Hotel. Dunn had the run of the town until the Harcourts gave him competition. He was a coward at heart and always carried a gun in his pocket.

Dunn sent word to "Silver Jack" that he needed a bartender but did not mention having a feud with the Harcourts. Luke and Jack had been chums "down below." When the latter took over his job at Dunn's, he naturally renewed his friendship with Luke and the brothers. He tended bar and took charge of the roughnecks who started anything. He was respected by everyone who knew him and a word from him quieted any trouble which started in the establishment.

One day Luke Harcourt and Jack were playing cards in the "snakeroom" of the saloon and got into an argument. Both men were well under the influence of liquor.

Luke, with the confidence which the solidarity the Harcourt brothers gave him, threw down his cards and told Jack that Dunn had brought him to Seney just to clean up his enemies, the Harcourts included. This accusation, that he was only a thug to strong-arm those who hated Dunn, came as a blow to Jack. He denied knowing anything about it and went into the bar and called Dunn. Throwing his bartender's apron in his face, stalked out of the place without demanding his pay.

This incident led to the shooting of two men, a prolonged prison sentence for another and a quieter life in Seney for a few months.

Jack returned to the lumber camps again and was looked upon as one of the best-all-round bosses in the Seney area. His last log drive was on the Yellow Dog River. He came to Seney to recruit a crew of river hogs and had no trouble skimming off the most skilled men about the town. Men liked to work for him, for he was fair and stopped any trouble which developed within the crew. When rival companies fought for flowage rights on the river, Jack could settle the matter with his fists and calked boots and the men wanted to witness these affairs, knowing that their side would win.

But years of dissipation and the term in Jackson Prison finally slowed the burly fellow down. He was still the champ to the people in that north country. During his time he possessed an insatiable lust for battle. He had mopped up the champions of the Lower Peninsula lumber camps and mill towns and was king across the Straits of Mackinac.

"Silver Jack" faded out of the picture gradually. He no longer frequented the camps or the streets about Seney. He turned up in Duluth where he tended bar for "Bull Dog" Hogan who ran a dance hall and sporting house where trouble could start at any time. Where there was trouble Jack seemed to be present. A bunch of the local rowdies, lumberjacks and roustabouts from the docks decided to clean out the place, wreck the furniture and drive "Bull Dog" and the girls out of town. But they figured without Driscoll. When the fight started and was going along at an interesting clip, "Silver Jack" wheeled in. When the fight was over there were men lying on the floor, unconscious, or sitting up against the walls feeling of their wounds.

One of the trouble makers was the member of a prominent Duluth family, which threatened to arrest Driscoll for beating up on their "boy." Silver Jack jumped to Superior, Wisconsin, the twin city across the bridge from Duluth. In Superior he became the foreman of a crew laying cedar block pavement, from which vantage point he could thumb his nose at the law across the state line.

The last appearance of "Silver Jack" was in far away L'Anse, the scene of the last big lumbering operations in western Upper Peninsula. It was on log drive that he fell into the icy water in the spring of 1895. Pneumonia developed and he was brought to the Ottawa Hotel operated by Belonger and his mother. A doctor was called and ordered him to bed. Jack joked about a little bug laying him low when not even "Frenchy" Fournier or Angus Bronson could keep him down.

On the evening of March 31, when Mrs. Belonger brought up his supper, he asked her that when she brought his breakfast the next morning to shout down the stairs that he was dead.

"Oliver will come running," he laughed, "and I'll scare the life out of him by rising up in bed and shouting 'April Fool.'"

The next morning when Mrs. Belonger brought up the meal, the fabulous "Silver Jack" Driscoll was dead. His April first joke died with him. Oliver, the simple-minded hotel flunky refused to enter the room of his dead friend. With tears streaming down his face, he ran down the streets of L'Anse shouting:

"Come queek, ev'ry bo-dy, the great 'Silver Jack,' she is dead!"

The champion was quietly buried in an unmarked grave with a few of his friends witnessing his last rites. His days of swash-buckling, drinking and fighting were over. Like Paul Bunyan, the tales of his exploits grew in proportion. His fame as a flesh and blood figure grew as the years passed, until today the oldtime lumberjacks recount in the many taverns in the U.P. almost fabulous stories of the famous, loved and notorious "Silver Jack" Driscoll.

Jack's fame was recorded in Charles B. Reilly's collection of lumberjack materials in the following verse:

"SILVER JACK"

I was on the drive in '80,
On the drive with Silver Jack;
He's in the penitentiary now,
But he's soon expected back.

There was a chap among us
By the name of Bobby Waite;
He was smooth, slick and cunning
As a college graduate.

He could talk on any subject,
From the Bible to Hoyle.
His words flew out as easy
As ever man poured oil.

He was what you call a skeptic,
And he loved to set and weave
His tales of fancy wonders
And things we couldn't believe.

One day, while waiting for a flood,
We all were settin' 'round
Smokin' Niggerhead tobacco
And hearing Bob expound.

He said Hell was all a humbug,
And he showed as plain as day
That the Bible was a fable
And how much it looked that way.

"You're a liar," someone shouted,
And you've got to take it back."
And everybody started,
'Twas the voice of "Silver Jack."

"Maybe I've not used the Lord
Always exactly white,
But when a champ abuses Him
He must eat his words or fight.

"It was in that old religion
That my mother lived and died;
Her memory's ever dear to me,
And I say that Bob has lied."

Now Bob he was no coward;
And he spoke up brave and free:
"Put up your dukes and fight, my lad,
You'll find no flies on me."

They fought for forty minutes
While the boys would whoop and cheer;
And Jack spit up a tooth or two
And Bobby lost an ear.

At last Jack got him underneath
And slugged with all his might;
So Bobby finally agreed
That Silver Jack was right.

And when they got through fighting
And rose up from the ground
A friend fished out a bottle
And it went quietly round.

They drank to Jack's religion
In a solemn sort of way
And just to clinch the argument
They worked no more that day.

CHAPTER EIGHTEEN

High Stakes at Cards

ALTHOUGH drinking, fighting and "loving" were the sensational highlights in the life of the lumberjacks at Seney, gambling was not often indulged in for high stakes. Leave that to the professionals in the big cities.

During the short evenings before the men in the camps turned into their straw-covered bunks card playing was a favorite pasttime. The stakes, if there were any, were usually a package of Peerless tobacco, a plug of chewing or a box of snuff. Basically honest, the woodsmen had few quarrels over cards and these differences of opinion were easily settled by the men who occupied the "deacon's seat," which was reserved for the men who had shown particular skill in the woods or leadership among the crew.

There were a few professional gamblers who went into the camps for the purpose of passing themselves off as woodsmen to engage in card gambling and winning from the less skilled players. No lumber company allowed gambling in their camps. Crews could be too easily disorganized by the quarrels that followed cheating at cards. Whenever a professional was discovered he was summarily dealt with by the bosses and the men themselves.

One such card shark, Jim Brady, worked in the camps in winter, barbered some in camp and acted as dealer in stud poker games when in town. One spring he applied for the job of poker dealer in the notorious Dan Dunn saloon. Dunn took him on. An exciting game began in the morning, continued all day long and into the late evening. Big stakes exchanged hands. Finally one of the players thought he discovered Brady dealing from the bottom of the deck. He asked for a recess in the game and took one of the other players out into the back room with him. Together they laid their plan. They returned to the room. One of them took a seat next to Brady and the other took a seat opposite the dealer.

The game proceeded and Brady was carefully watched by the pair. The gambler was seen dealing slyly from the bottom of the deck again. The first player, with a quick shove, upset the table onto Brady and called him a damned cheat. The chum shot out the kerosene lamp overhead, throwing the room into darkness and confusion. The pair made for Brady, who knowing that he had been caught at cheating, dodged behind the heating stove to the door, out behind the saloon bar and into the street through the swinging doors and down the sidewalk. Several shots were fired at him but none struck him in his flight.

Brady left Seney in the darkness and no word was heard of him for two years. The card room lamps were relighted and the wreck cleared. Over three hundred dollars were found on the floor and was divided between the four remaining players and the bartender. Two years later one of the men entered a barbershop in Duluth and found Brady shaving a customer. The gambler admitted to him that the Seney game was the last card game he had played in.

THE LOGGING TRAIN

When river driving was unprofitable logging railroads were built into the pine stands to haul logs to the sawmill.

It was other than lumberjacks who carried on the gambling which went on in Seney. The few dollars the woodsmen and river drivers had left over after a winter in the forest and a few days of free spending in town were not enough to attract professional gamblers. There were a few self-confessed card sharks who sought to outguess the gamblers and these one-sided contests under the kerosene lamps and around the rough tables in the card rooms tingled the blood of those who sought tense excitement.

A pair of Finns started a game of poker with two native lumberjacks. Though the stakes were small, the local men kept losing every hand. The Finns kept up a running chatter in their own tongue. Suddenly one of the other players became suspicious.

"Why, in hell, don't you Finns talk United States?"

Innocently, one of the Finns replied in English:

"I was just asking him if he had any spades."

The American lumberjacks promptly kicked over the table and drove their Finnish opponents out of the saloon.

The gambling fever which had struck the professional and would-be professionals in the early days recurred from time to time when some of the local boys got together with the cardboards.

John J. Riordan, the present station agent for the D. S. S. & A. railroad at Seney, who came on the job as a twenty year old stripling in 1916 to be the railroad telegrapher, relates what he saw during the first few days in his new position.

Riordan came to Seney long after the lumbering business had reached its peak but when the town still lived up to some of its early traditions of reckless living and abandon. The big woods operations were over but a few companies were still picking up the stray and overlooked stands of pine and hardwoods in the vicinity. The town had already taken on the appearance of a ghost village. A number of the old buildings and homes had been abandoned. Grass had begun to grow on some of the back streets and the roads which led to the closed camps. Growths of jack pine were creeping closer and closer to the dying lumber town.

The incumbent station agent met Riordan at the incoming train and took him to the hotel where he met the drunken manager and secured an upstairs room. At the railroad station there had been a drunken party going on all night. The station agent, a conductor and two brakesmen were riotous in their cups.

Below Riordan's quarters, in the room next to the barroom, a poker game was in progress. The loud voices of the players and the on-lookers and the pounding on the table kept Riordan from sleeping. He dressed again and went down to see what was going on. The game continued far into the night. At one time there was a total of $6000.00 in stakes on the table. In the morning the station agent had a desperate hangover. He asked Riordan to take over the selling of tickets to the passengers coming in and going out of Seney, lumberjacks, traveling men and a few "fancy ladies."

Saturday morning the poker game started up again with upwards of $4000.00 on the table. The hotel proprietor, the station agent, a teamster, two camp foremen and a traveling man sat around the table, with a ring of spectators about them. The game continued all day. The bartender supplied sandwiches and beer. Riordan worked at the station all day and all night again. The next morning when he dropped in at the hotel, the men were still slapping down their cards and pushing their red, white and blue chips into the center of the table. The bartender had been kept busy and the men were well jagged.

The station agent gave Riordan the combination to the station safe in order to continue to sell tickets and make change. Monday morning the agent staggered into the depot clutching $300.00 in bills, which was his take from three days and three nights of gambling. He paid Riordan for his three day and three night vigil at the station out of his earnings.

CHAPTER NINETEEN

The Undoing of Dan Dunn

DAN DUNN had been one of the most notorious characters and law breakers in the Upper Peninsula for many years. His reputation as a bad man, a bully and desperado was known far and wide wherever lumbermen gathered. He was a contradictory individual, who neither drank, gambled or used profanity. He was known to have bought a Bible for his mother, the best leather-bound copy available, from a traveling book salesman. He resembled a banker more than a saloon keeper as he stood behind his bar, peering across the street through heavily lidded eyes and bushy eyebrows.

Dunn contributed more than any one individual or all the rough lumberjacks to the bad name of Seney, which the town and its inhabitants could never verify or suppress. He had fled a bench warrant "down Roscommon way" and joined other fugitives and lawbreakers to this "port of missing men" to which Detroit sent its unclaimed mail. At Roscommon he operated a saloon and a bawdy house or "hoodlum". Hailed before the courts repeatedly, he escaped a jail sentence or fine. He was a power in politics but at heart a coward. His six-shooter was always present on his person. With a character called Mahoney he operated his stockade and was said to have kept vicious dogs to prevent the inmates from escaping, although the story of stockades and dogs was often repeated but never verified. Dick Anger was his "boss pimp".

Some of the Harcourt brothers, of whom there were six, Tom, Luke, Jim, Dick, Bill and Steve, operated a saloon in Roscommon and a feud between them and Dunn sprang up, which was settled only by the shooting of young Steve at Seney and Dunn at Trout Lake.

When the rousing town of Roscommon became too hot for Dunn and he was in danger of the long-defied law, it was said that he took everything removable from his saloon and hired an old chronic drunk for $50.00 to set fire to the building. Between them they filled the place with empty wooden boxes to give the appearance of it being well stocked. The old drunk did a complete job in Dunn's absence and Dunn was able to collect the fire insurance to finance in part his Seney venture. He also borrowed heavily from a Roscommon druggist. He built a saloon in Seney and a "hoodlum" up the Driggs River a few miles from Seney.

A few years thereafter the firebug followed Dunn to Seney and blackmailed him repeatedly for money to keep him quiet. Dunn always refused to give him money when he was drunk for fear that liquor would loosen his tongue.

According to Tom Harcourt, who with his brothers, had moved to Seney and opened the White House Hotel and a saloon, two lumberjacks saw Dunn talking with the firebug. They heard Dunn ask the old fellow if he would assist him in running some lines on a forty acre tract of land north of Seney which Dunn planned to buy. This land was covered by a dense growth of tamarack, poplar and jackpine. The two listeners, thinking it was peculiar

The Wanigan
or Cook Float
on the Spring
Drive

A Gala Evening in Camp

The Christmas Sleigh Ride

A Friendly
Game of Cards

(Courtesy Mrs. Marie Robbins from 54-year-old photos)

that Dunn would engage an old sot to assist him in this accurate work, followed the pair, keeping concealed in the thick growth. As Dunn and his victim stopped within a thicket of jackpine, the men crept closer to hear what Dunn was saying. He was pointing at an object ahead of the old man. As he turned to see what Dunn was pointing at, the latter pulled out a large revolver and shot the old man through the back. Dunn examined the body and returned to his pinery dive and brought back a shovel. The watchers saw him dig a grave in the soft sand and bury his victim.

The two men were afraid to tell the authorities about the cold-blooded affair for fear that Dunn would hear about them and polish them off in the same way. They hurriedly left Seney and did not return for several years, when they had learned about Dunn's death and reported the incident.

The unpaid loan from the Roscommon druggist came up to haunt Dunn. His creditor wrote him repeatedly asking for payments but Dunn ignored his appeals. As time went on the druggist became more and more demanding and finally threatened to sue Dunn.

The bawdy house operator had acquired some land in the great swamp surrounding Seney where bog iron ore lay close to the surface. Believing that he may have struck upon a lucrative find, Dunn set some workmen to dig a large, long hole on an island in the swamp and bring some of the ore to the surface and spread it around the diggings. He had the ore analized and found that it contained fifty-five percent metallic iron but not in sufficient quantities to merit mining it.

When the Roscommon druggist suddenly appeared on

the scene to collect the long standing debt, Dunn told him about his rich discovery and offered to give the Roscommon man a share in exchange for the loan. Together they went to the pit. Pointing to the hole and the bog ore laying on the surface, Dunn remarked:—

"There's where your money went. I sunk it in that find of good ore".

As the druggist stepped down the hole to examine the diggings, Dunn shot him through the head and buried him under the red stuff.

These gruesome stories circulated about Seney for several years without verification until the two lumberjacks returned after Dunn's death to lead Tom Harcourt and John Bellaire to the now overgrown hole where they unearthed what remained of the druggist. Only the leg and arm bones and skull were left, deeply stained with the red iron ore.

The Harcourt family originated in Ireland and were a fearless lot who would fight "at the drop of a hat". The brothers were loyal to each other to a great degree. They were well liked by the people of the community, honest and trustworthy, but with a burning hatred for Dunn. They, like Dunn, were active in politics and had rival saloons. The feud, which had begun in Roscommon, was kept at a red heat when they moved to Seney. Everyone knew that the bad blood between them had reached a stage where violent bloodshed was a natural consequence. It was about that time that Dunn had hired "Silver Jack" Driscoll as a bartender to put his rivals in their places. One day as Luke Harcourt and Driscoll were engaged in a friendly game of cards, one of them made a misplay and a quarrel started. Luke told Jack off for being hired by

Dunn to clean up on the Harcourt brothers. This was news to Jack, who immediately took the matter to Dunn and quit his job on the spot. Deprived of his strongarm bouncer, Dunn threatened to shoot any Harcourt on sight.

Few residents were abroad in Seney on Saturday, June 25, 1891, to see Steve Harcourt enter the saloon of Dan Dunn, the overlord of lawlessness in what was known as the wildest and wide-open town in Michigan. Steve had returned the evening before with his family from a camping trip up the river. Perhaps just on a dare, the twenty year old youngster entered Dunn's saloon and ordered a drink and one for the men in the place. Dunn refused to give a god-damned Harcourt a drink in his saloon. Steve then told Dunn off for his many crimes and lawlessness. As the argument got heated Dunn struck Steve over the head with a whiskey bottle, shattering the bottle. Then reaching under the bar he pulled out a gun and shot Steve through the jaw.

Steve tried to get his gun out of his pocket but was hampered by having it wrapped in a red handkerchief. His shot at Dunn struck the top of the bar, ricocheted and drove through the middle of a painting of John L. Sullivan hung on the backbar mirror. Dunn's second shot struck Steve's side. He staggered out of the door. Here his eight year old nephew, knowing that something was happening to his favorite uncle, had come running. The boy took the bleeding man by the hand and led him into his home where he lay down. Steve's mother picked glass out of his skull and sent the boy for the doctor. Steve lived only two or three days.

Dunn was arrested for manslaughter and at a preliminary hearing in Manistique was discharged,—no cause for action — justified homocide in self-defense. This was Dunn's fourth arrest and fourth discharge for a serious crime. The free use of money and his connection with county officials were given as the reason for his acquittal. Now fearful of revenge at the hands of the remaining Harcourts, Dunn and his wife left Seney on their way to Canada. They planned to return later to take up their notorious occupation. Dunn had sworn out a warrant for the arrest of the Harcourts to keep the peace.

It was said that the brothers held a council and drew straws to decide which of them would revenge their brother's death. Jim drew the short straw.

County Sheriff Dennis Heffron made the trip to Seney to serve the papers on the Harcourts. They offered no resistance. They accompanied the officer peacefully. At Trout Lake they were to change trains. There was time for a drink at the saloon of Jack Nevens, a friend of both the Harcourts and Dunn. Dunn and his wife were staying with the Nevens family in the flat above the saloon, enroute to Manistique to be present at the hearing of the keep-peace warrant. When Nevens saw the sheriff and the Harcourts emerge from the train, he advised Dunn to stay out of the saloon and not show himself until the next train pulled out. Dunn saw the men come into the saloon from his upstairs room, put his gun in his coat pocket and came down into the barroom. He was standing at the end of the bar talking with Nevens when he looked into the mirror and saw the brothers coming through the front door.

Dunn reached into his pocket for his gun. Jim Harcourt, who had drawn the short straw, saw the move and quicker than sight whipped out his gun and fired four

135

shots into Dunn's body before it fell to the barroom floor. The first shot struck him through the heart. Jim turned and gave himself up to the sheriff. The officer took the gun which Dunn still clasped in his hand.

The shooting took place in Trout Lake, which is in Chippewa county. The Schoolcraft county Sheriff Heffron wired the Chippewa county sheriff, who took Jim Harcourt to Sault Ste. Marie for trial.

When the case was tried a few months later half of the population of Seney was present in the courtroom. Feeling ran high. Men and women on the streets of the Soo argued over the merits of the case, most of them contending that Jim Harcourt's deed deserved a bounty and not a prison sentence. Ironically, Dunn, whose money had influenced other juries in the past, had his revenge even in death. The jury found Jim guilty and the judge sentenced him to seven and a half years in Marquette State Prison.

Before the judge pronounced sentence he asked Jim whether he had any statement to make.

"Yes, your honor," he said quietly. "I'm sure that Dunn will not kill me or any more of my brothers."

A model prisoner, Jim served only three years of his sentence. His wife and hundreds of friends circulated a petition for his release, claiming therein that Jim Harcourt had rendered a service to the county and the state by removing the "Northern Peninsula Terror" and that Jim should have been pensioned for life rather than sent to prison for his deed.

Through Tom Touey of Bay City, a friend of Jim, James T. Hurst, a state representative in the Michigan legislature and an attorney, influenced the governor to grant Harcourt a pardon at the end of three years.

A great celebration was staged when Jim returned to Seney by the people who loved him. He was soon elected supervisor which office he held for nine terms. He was elected deputy sheriff for six years, serving under Sheriff Klagster. John Baird, Michigan conservation chief, appointed him conservation officer for Schoolcraft county, where he served for two years.

After the turn of the century and after Seney was but a grass-grown village again, Jim and his wife and three sons and three daughters moved to more peaceful scenes in southern Michigan. He honored Representative Hurst by naming one of his stalwart sons for him. He bought property at Houghton Lake and operated a large gravel business there until the time of his death.

Several days after Dunn's unmourned death and funeral, a number of Seney women were gathered at the O'Brien home directly across from the infamous Dunn saloon. As they were visiting and recalling the shooting, Nellie Ryan, the former Nellie Harcourt and sister of Jim, saw flames of fire within the saloon. The place was burning down. As they looked they noticed a rocking chair moving to and fro, evidently fanned by the breeze created by the flames.

"Look," she said. "See that chair moving. That's Dan Dunn's soul rocking in hell!"

CHAPTER TWENTY

P. K. Small and the Pot Hill Gang

Gᴏᴅ, there were some awful men around here in those days", claimed Roy Curry, who as a railroad engineer had hauled billions of feet of pine over the logging railroads about Seney in those burly times. "And P. K. Small was one of the worst", he added.

P.K. was a precocious pain in the gluteus maximum of the law enforcement officers. Never dangerous, he continually got into minor scrapes from which he had to be extricated. He was one of the colorful, repulsive men who inhabited every pioneer community. He had come from the Saginaw Valley lumber camps and was an unwashed, crafty and unlovely individual. The waning Saginaw lumber region no longer held enough excitement to satisfy his restless and venturesome spirit, so Seney, Michigan's small hell on earth, was his logical destination.

Small had been in many rough and tumble fights down Saginaw way and had had his nose bitten off. Only two holes remained of what had been his inquisitive probosis which had poked into other people's affairs too many times. His face was well marked with "lumberjack smallpox". He was never known to have washed his face or taken a bath. His·only dunking occured when he fell off a rolling log on the spring drive.

The clothes this character wore were typically lumberjack,—a plaid wool shirt, caked with grime and sweat at the collar and sleeve cuffs, open at the neck; his heavy woolen underwear which he wore the year around showed black at the sleeve ends and was fastened by a horse-blanket pin across his chest. His felt hat had once been black, but now it was mildewed grey, torn at the band and greasy from sweat and dust. His baggy woolen pants were cut off at the middle of the calf, shiny with grease and gave him the appearance of preparing to jump. His once broad, red suspenders crossed his muscular back and were fastened to his pants by whittled pieces of pine for buttons. His leather hightop boots joined the bottom of his stag pants at the middle of his calves and were run down at the heels and pigeon-toed, the calks worn to mere stubs of their original sharp selves. These calks had kicked the body and face of his antagonists many times over his many years in the camps and towns.

Small worked in the woods when he needed money badly but his favorite rendezvous was the lively town of Seney where he spent most of the year mooching drinks from the flush lumberjacks, the barkeepers and from gullible visitors and traveling men. He ate lunch at the end of the bars when he was hungry. He lived by his wits, his fists and by his penchant for playing practical jokes on the innocents.

One of P.K.'s favorite tricks was to watch for a "dude" getting off the trains. Sneaking up behind him, he would grab his victim by the middle, turn him upside down and shake the loose change and other valuables from his pockets. Then collecting this "loose offering", as he called it, he would head for the nearest saloon, followed by the on-lookers, and buy the drinks for the crowd. The men

WILKES HARGRAVE
started his bank by shaving P. K. Small with a jacknife. He left a
half million dollar estate to be squandered by his progeny.

knew that wherever P.K. was there would be excitement and a few free drinks.

Another character, Paddy Joice, joined P.K. in some of his escapades. Together they made up the most successful moochers and practical jokers in those parts. Their methods were innumerable and original.

One day one of the habitues of Dunn's tavern plied P.K. and Paddy with whiskey and gave them a useless, rusty revolver and dared them to hold up the passengers on the noon D.S.S.&A. train. Small and Joice boarded the train as it pulled in, one from each end of the single passenger coach, brandished their revolver and ordered the passengers to hold up their hands. Women fainted and men cowered behind seats. One of the men passengers noted the condition of the pair as they staggered down the car and saw the rusty weapon. He stuck his foot into the aisle and tripped Joice and knocked the revolver out of P.K.'s hand.

The two derilicts were booted off the train and collared by the town marshall. They were each given ninety days in jail for their prank. The instigator went free.

When there were no dudes to shake down, Small would go out into the street and pick a fight. He knew how to handle himself and was seldom bested. In the struggle P.K. would reach his hand into his victim's pocket and extract what money he had. If his victim proved to be a tougher man than he thought, he would resort to the manly art of earchewing. Dr. Bohn had sewed up several ears upon which P.K. had operated with his yellow teeth. When a jack appeared in a saloon with a pair of "shiners" and was asked how he had accumulated them he replied:

"Oh, P.K. was passing them around today and I took

a pair."

As free drinks and free lunches became harder to get and he had exhausted all his favorite trick to secure these necessities, Small became the first snake-eater in those parts. Entering a saloon with a harmless grass snake in his clutches, he would offer to bit off its head for a glass of whiskey. He used frogs in the same manner.

According to Roy Curry, P.K. and a chum entered a brothel located on the banks of the Tahquamenon River a mile north of Eckerman. Small had a thin dime left in his grimy pants pocket and bought each of them a glass of beer which would also entitle them to a free lunch. The inmates of the place had a pet crow which would fly from shoulder to shoulder and peck away at ears. It landed on P.K.'s shoulder as he was about to drink his beer. Annoyed at this interference, he reached his ugly face around and bit the crow's head off. He spit the head into his glass and drank the beer with the crow's blood with it. He was promptly kicked out by the "madam" and refused admittance thereafter.

The next winter P.K. was really "on the bum." Work in the woods was scarce. The men who found no employment were at the mercy of their friends and the hardhearted saloon keepers. No one would give P.K. free lunches or free drinks any longer. His foul reputation had closed the gates of mercy. He was kicked out of place after place. Yet life was still sweet to him. He was not ready to go to his happy hunting ground, for he hadn't raised enough hell and his career as a notorious troublemaker was far from the end. He was still to live a long life of minor crime and sin.

He entered Martin's saloon at Eckerman from which

he had been forcibly ejected many times and asked for a free lunch or a small piece of change to buy food. Everyone turned the filthy man down. Turning to his erstwhile friends of better days, he flung out:

"God damn it, if you SOBs won't give me something to eat, I know where I can get it."

With this he walked out of the saloon and into the street where teams of horses were tied. Stooping down, he picked up a handful of fresh horse drippings and ate them before the onlookers. Someone told Mrs. Martin about the incident. She came into the saloon and berated her husband, then invited P.K. into her kitchen where she would feed him. Turning to his tormenters, he shouted:

"To hell with all you SOBs around this town of Eckerman. I'll go back to Seney and see "Dad" O'Brien. He'll feed me. At least he'll have some of his pork left."

Small's greatest achievement in his colorful and notorious career in the Seney district was his organization of the famous Pot Hill Gang. On a low sandy mound of earth thrown up by the glaciers and surrounded by a swamp, the Manistique Lumber Company had erected a small set of camps, just north of Seney. When the boom days had passed the camps were abandoned and left to rot. A mysterious fire destroyed all but one of the log buildings. P. K. was suspected of having done the job out of revenge for his shabby treatment in town.

The remaining building became the rendezvous for the hard-luck lumberjacks who had spent their winter and spring wages on whiskey, gambling and women. It was here where P.K., with his sharp wits, ruthless methods and his ability to fight all comers, became the cock-of-the-walk and the King of the Pot Hill Gang. It was here where from twenty to fifty men tided themselves over the slim summer months until the camps called them back to work in the fall.

The jungle men slept in the log building, washed their clothes in a nearby creek, and lived off the country. Deer in their red summer coats were plentiful in the woods and the Fox River teemed with speckled trout—both to be had for the taking. From their vantage point near Seney the Pot Hill Gang had no difficulty in procuring food. The people of the town kept chickens, pigs and cattle and raised vegetable gardens.

P.K. and his boys would simply walk into town and make their demands on the residents and invariably brought back ample provisions. The townspeople knew that if they did not contribute voluntarily, their animals and vegetables would disappear in the night. Since stock was allowed to roam freely through the woods and fields seeking forage, it was an easy matter for some of them to become "lost". "Dad" O'Brien never did know how many of his wandering hogs fell into the clutches of the Gang.

P.K., Billy Kennedy and Paddy Marvin, "The Boston Kid", were the chicken specialists. Their method was to bait a fishline with corn, drop the line over a chicken fence and hook their supply of fowl. At night they had an even more ingenious scheme. They would approach a chicken coop, knock out a pane of glass, then reach their arms inside, place it along the pole where the chickens were roosting and wait. Soon the chickens, feeling the warm arm, would step onto it and roost. Then the thieves would withdraw their arms and the chickens, stuff them into a sack and take them back to the Gang.

When a company supply team came along the road, the Gang would highjack the load to obtain flour, sugar and beans. The lumber company finally gave their supply teamsters orders to let the Gang have what it wanted, for it knew that if this was not done the Gang would demand even more than was offered.

Order in the Gang was established under P.K.'s able management. There was an unwritten code of law (few could read or write) which functioned inexorably. Should one of the boys be caught stealing from another member, quick justice followed. There was no jury trial to allow the thief to get off easily because of the sympathy of his friends. P.K. was the prosecutor, judge and jury. Justice was quick and harsh. Sentences varied from hard labor, doing the cooking, making beds, washing clothes for the others, to cutting firewood or whatever came into P.K.'s mind at the time. If the offender was found guilty of a second offense against the Gang, he was more severly punished. "Watering" meant stripping him of his clothes and driving him across the Fox River under a lash. Tarring and feathering was for the most serious crimes. Second offenses were rare, for the Gang knew what would follow. For the third offense, the rules held, death could be inflicted, but this was never enforced. P.K. was King, who provided for his subjects and they were loyal to him. The Gang lived at the Hill until snow began to fly, then set off to lumber camps for the winter.

One fall after P.K. had been on a "bender" for several weeks, he decided to go back to the woods, which meant looking for work in a lumber camp. By this time his work clothes were badly torn in his many fights and caked with mud from sleeping on the ground in drunken stupors. Wilkes Hargrove, a newcomer to the wild town, had just opened a general store. P.K. decided that Hargrove would be an "easy touch". While he was looking over the items he would like to buy on credit—a mackinaw, mittens, long-handled underwear, wool pants, rubber-soled shoes, plug tobacco, shirts, socks, etc., he remarked to Hargrove, rubbing his grizzled beard:

"Jeez, I'd give a dollar for a shave."

Hargrove stepped out from behind the counter and said:

"Just step into the back room and I'll give you a shave for a dollar."

The storekeeper, anxious to make his first dollar, brought out a tin cup of cold water, a bar of yellow laundry soap and a sharp jackknife. He lathered P.K.'s face with the strong soap and scraped off the tough whiskers until tears rolled down P.K.'s face. But game to the last and never a man to admit defeat, he handed Hargrove his last silver dollar and departed with his purchases. Hargrove's dream of becoming a successful business man began to take on reality. He had made his first dollar. This silver dollar he kept until he had accumulated enough money to start his own bank in the store.

For years Hargrove catered to the lumber trade and the farmers in the area, made loans at high rates of interest, taking mortgages on lumbering equipment, farms and livestock as security. While his private banking ventures were never quoted on the New York Stock Exchange, at the time of his death he left his heirs a half million dollar estate, which was soon squandered by his profligate son, and his widow was buried at public ex-

147

pense. The big safe in which he kept his money is still in the general store in Seney and was in perfectly useable condition until a few years ago when a safe cracker from a big city cracked it open and destroyed its usefulness. But long before this Hargrove had accumulated the fortune started by P.K.'s dollar shave. The same front door through which P.K. carried his bundle of lumberjack clothes still swings open to present day customers of the original Hargrove general store.

P.K. Small lost his front teeth in fights and accidents, so he had trouble chewing his food. In his pocket he carried a sharp jackknife which he used to cut his meat wherever he ate in the camps, restaurants and hotels. Before eating he would pull out the knife and a small whetstone and proceed to sharpen the knife in the presence of all the patrons. One day in a Seney boarding house one of the jacks filched his knife and P.K. had a hard time with his meat. Not one to give up in the face of obstacles, he stuffed the meat into his shirt front and took it out into the woodshed and chopped it up with a hatchet.

The last news of the incredible P.K. Small came from Duluth, where, according the Roy Curry, the King of the Pot Hill Gang met an ignominious death in a fight in a saloon.

Fabulous, incredible as these tales of old P.K. may seem to modern civilized man, there are many oldtimers living today who tell of having known him in his heyday. They still recall how P.K. boasted that when he bought a ticket at Saginaw to go to Seney, he merely told the ticket agent that:—

"I want a ticket to hell."

That's how he landed in Seney!

CHAPTER TWENTY-ONE

It Was a Rugged Life

Eᴅ Cookson came to Seney from the lumber camps of Maine in 1878 after the pine in that state had been slashed off and floated down the Penobscot and the Androscoggin Rivers to the mills. Young and somewhat experienced in lumber camp technique, he sought a job in the Upper Peninsula with the Chicago Lumber Company, one of the largest operators in the Manistique area.

Cookson's initiation into the life of the new community was not entirely a pleasant one. He first secured lodging at the company hotel and boarding house. The hostelry had been leased only a few days before by John McCarthy who took Cookson to a little room on the upper floor of the frame building.

After he had crawled into the creaky wooden bed and had drawn the rough woolen blankets over him, his skin was afflicted with a burning sensation. As he scratched the burning increased. He jumped out of bed, recognizing the cause of this strange "fever" from his previous experiences in the lumber camps of Maine.

Striking a sulphur match, he lighted the kerosene lamp on the wooden stand and threw back the blankets. The covers and mattress were literally crawling with great, granddaddy bedbugs. He spent a miserable night. By bundling himself tightly in his long underwear and lying on top of the blankets, the young woodsman was able to get a little rest from the onslaught of the bedbug battalion.

McCarthy apologized the next morning for the presence of the vermin. He explained that he had just taken over the place and had not had time to scour the rooms with kerosene and fumigate with sulphur fumes.

Despite the fact that he realized what he would be in for in the lice and bedbug infested log buildings of the camps, he hired out as a teamster, hauling great loads of logs over the ice from the skidways to the river bank. Some of the older men in the camp resented the idea of the young "greenhorn" pulling down a well-paying job the first time he struck camp. They tried several ingenious methods to discourage him from staying the winter and told him exaggerated tales of terribly cold weather in that north country during January and February.

"I don't believe you'll be able to stand the cold out here this winter. You had better go south or back to Maine," said Millard Duell, a rugged, bearded oldtimer, who had not heard that Maine winters were even more severe than the climate that the U.P. afforded.

"How cold does she get up here?" asked Cookson, tongue in cheek.

"Boy, it sure gets terribly cold. I remember when we were building that bridge acrost the Manistique River the ice was so thick that it was scraping the bottom of the river bed and piled up the stones as it shoved along. It was so doggoned cold that if you flung a cup of water in the air it would freeze afore it hit the ground."

"Is that only how cold she gets here?" replied Cookson in distain. "Why, back in that state of Maine it gets

MICHIGAN'S "LIMITLESS" PINE

Pine was thought to be inexhaustible but in two decades only barren wasteland remained.

Burton Historical Collections.

so cold that if you toss a cup of boiling water into the air, it freezes before it hits the ground. I remember one winter it got so cold that the Penobscot River froze clear to the bottom over the whole length of the river. Not a drop of water moved until the spring thaw. Then the whole chunk of ice forty miles long moved out into the mouth of the river so that boats couldn't cross it until the next fall. Why, in cook camp that winter the steam from the tea kettle would freeze and drop back into the kettle to get warm again. The cook had to use blasting caps to get enough meat from the frozen beef to feed the men."

That settled the question of U.P. winters.

The winter of 1898 was generally rated as the coldest on record. The temperature remained as low as thirty-five degrees below zero for weeks at a time. The men's beards wore icicles inches long and had to be broken off from time to time to enable the men to swing their axes. Their beards, hair and caps wore a halo of frost while their clothing became stiff with cold. The horses' hides were caked with frost from end to end and the black, grey and bay horses became white until teamsters had difficulty in recognizing their own teams.

At one of the camps the sprinkler sleigh stopped to fill up with water to ice the roads. The ice was twenty-four inches thick and had to be chopped free to allow the barrel to enter the water hole. As the barrel descended from the top of the sprinkler, one of the men was knocked into the hole. Teamster, Mike Ferguson, pulled him out. The jack yelled in anger:—

"Why in hell did you have to pull me out? That water is a damned-site warmer than the air."

The men of the woods were skilled with the peavey, the double-bitted ax and the decking line but money flowed through their fingers like water. Once back in town after a grueling winter in the forest, they had no restraint over their winter's stake. Drinking, treating and paying back debts soon found them penniless.

From previous experience some found that if they left part of their cash with one of the stores, it lasted longer than if they left it with a tavern or in the hands of a saloon keeper. At times Bellaire had twenty or thirty men leave amounts from twenty-five to one hundred dollars with him for safekeeping at the store, with instructions to dole it out in fives and tens whenever they called for it. This money the clerk kept in a separate drawer in separate envelopes with each man's name and the amount deposited and withdrawn written thereon.

One lumberjack left $70.00 with instructions to give it to him in small amounts as he needed it but added that if he came in drunk and asked for money not to give him any. The fellow kept drawing small amounts until he had $45.00 left. One day he came in greatly intoxicated and asked for more. In his condition, there would be trouble if he were refused. Bellaire told him that all of his money was used up. The man turned toward the door and said:—

"All right," and staggered out of the store.

Two weeks later he came into the store and told Bellaire a hardluck story, relating what a fool he had made of himself for spending all of his cash. He now needed an outfit of clothes and other items in order to return to the woods. He asked Bellaire if he would trust him for $15.00's worth, which Bellaire agreed to do. This was a complete surprise to the jack, for the stores had recently carried no charge accounts because of the habitual drifting of the men from town to town.

He was completely outfitted but kept bemoaning his foolishness.

"You're not as bad off as you think," Bellaire told him. "You still have $30.00 in the store safe after you pay for this bill. I followed your instruction and kept you from spending it all in the saloons.

"Whoopee, give me the balance!"

He wanted to stop buying clothes, draw out the balance and put it into circulation again. Bellaire refused to accomodate him and the jack wanted to start a fight. At last he was outfitted and Bellaire gave him enough money to pay off his board bill plus a week's board in advance to tide him over until the camp opened. That gave him a home. His credit was reestablished. He went on a protracted spree. The clothes were marked with his name and left in the store under the counter. He did not call for them for two weeks, when he was down and out again and had no alternative but to return to his camp.

"Damn ye, come back wit' me cap, you bloody bigger!"

Big Jim McGraw was shouting and shaking his huge boney fist at a great owl which had dropped out of a nearby tree in the Seney swamp and lifted off his headgear and carried it off into the deep woods.

A roar of laughter came up from the Driggs River where Jim Carney and Jack Skidmore were unloading sleighs of logs for George Hovey. McGraw strode away in impotent rage, resenting the laughter as well as the loss of his grey wool cap.

McGraw was not the only victim of the owl on that clear, frosty morning back in the year of 1905. Six other lumberjacks had lost their caps as the strange, wide-winged bird swooped down noiselessly out of the trees of the swamp and snatched off their headpieces.

The crew had just arrived at the scene of the work when the humorous antics of the owl took place. The sleigh haul was through a deep cedar swamp. McGraw and George Burke were walking on the road to start loading the sleighs. Burke became the second victim. He not only lost his cap but the sharp talons of the bird cut a deep gash in his ear. Bill Allen, the timber fitter, and Phil Prendergast, a road monkey, also had their caps swiped from their heads. A little Austrian from Manistique nearly had the wits scared out of him when the owl carried his cap into the dark underbrush.

After three other men lost their headgear, they decided to end the marauding habits of the strange bird. Jay Hunt brought his rifle along the next morning. Hiding himself out of sight of the tree from which the owl had come but in full view of the woods workers, he waited. As the men came on the scene and began their work, the owl, with his four foot wingspread, glided noiselessly from the deep foliage directly at the first man in the clearing. Hunt raised his rifle and cocked the hammer. The bird swooped down and carried off the gray cap from off the man's head. As it began its flight back to the woods, Hunt drilled it with a bullet. Its cap snitching days were over.

Only three of the men recovered their caps which they found at the foot of the tree where the owl had roosted. Apparently it had thought the caps were either rabbits or partridge on which it was in the habit of feasting. A cap moving about the snow on the top of a woodsman's head was not unlike a moving prey.

Alex McKinnon was lost on a dark night in an alcoholic fog as he stumbled from Dunn's saloon on his way home to his shack in the woods. Hardly knowing the direction he was taking, he crossed Boot Hill, the cemetery at the edge of Seney where homeless lumberjacks were buried.

A newly dug grave yawned across his path and he stumbled in. Sobering up a bit, he struggled to climb out of the deep hole but the sand and gravel kept rolling down on him as he clawed to get up. He yelled for help. Joe Mafraw was walking along the road past the cemetery and heard the yelling and cursing. He walked carefully toward the sound. He came to the open grave and called:

"Who's there?"

"It's me, Alex McKinnon. I can't get out of this damned hole."

"Why don't you stay there then?"

"It's too cold down here."

"No wonder you're cold. You've kicked off all the dirt they shoveled over you!"

Lumberjacks were a hardy lot. Accustomed to below zero weather while working knee deep in the woods, their bodies could withstand rigors which would have overcome a city man. Their wounds healed rapidly and their broken bones knitted much more quickly than those of other men. Frequently a jack would fall from a second story window or from a hotel balcony while intoxicated and suffer no hurt. Their bodies seemed to relax like that of a baby. After they recovered their lost "wind,"

156

they arose and headed for their destination as though nothing had happened.

Joe Donner of Seney was on his way to camp with a "load" under his belt. He tried to negotiate a small creek and fell into the icy water. Stunned, he lay there until the water froze him in. The next morning he was found by one of the men who chopped him out. He carried Joe's stiff body to the nearest house and called the coroner to come bury him. Before the coroner arrived Joe was thawed out and alive again and ready to walk to the camp.

Jim Lynch was head push on a spring drive. He was a good woodsman but this was his first job in charge of driving logs down a turbulant river. A ten mile jam had formed on the river. It appeared that the logs would stay there until the headwater had passed down the river and leave the logs hung up dry. Joe Curry and Fred Gonier, two experienced river men, were in charge of that particular spot on the river and were having a hard time with the miles of piled up logs.

Lynch came up from down below and started an argument with Joe and Fred as to how the jam should be handled. In the heat of the argument Joe told Lynch to "get the hell out of here" or he'd throw him over the dam. Lynch took off hurriedly. Soon the jam was broken and millions of feet of logs were hurtling down stream, plunging, rolling and booming with such great force that the noise could be heard miles away.

Lynch came running up the river and berated Joe and Fred:

"Why in hell did you break so much of the jam? Why didn't you stop part of it before it got away?"

Joe cocked his head at Lynch and replied with a grin: "Why in hell didn't you stop it down the river where you were?"

Camp clerks, timber estimaters, scalers and anyone who used a pencil in the camps were looked upon by the lowly lumberjacks as "educated" men. Few of the men could read or write. Some depended upon the educated men to write their letters and read their mail.

Bill Dunbar, the timber estimator for one of the outfits, needed a waterproof contained for his record books which he carried with him on his long trips through the timber estimating the future cut. He had the camp harness repairman sew straps to two large baking powder cans so he could carry his records in them. The straps fitted over his shoulder and the cans hung at his side. There was much speculation among the men as to what Dunbar carried in his cans. Lumberjacks were a suspicious lot and their guesses as to the contents of Dunbar's containers were many and far off the mark.

One afternoon as Dunbar approached a decking place in the woods carrying his baking powder cans, "Bughouse" McCarthy called out to the men around him:

"What in hell does Dunbar carry in them cans?"

Up spoke "Utica" Tom:

"Judgment, you damn fool, judgment!"

Con Kilrane ran camps and a railroad logging road of his own and always paid his men off in hard cash. No time slips or checks for him. He made a small fortune and always kept his business to himself. When asked one spring by a friend how much money he had made by his winter's operation, he replied:

"Two kegs. Two kegs."

SENEY'S FIRST BASEBALL TEAMS

Rivalry between towns was keen and rough. Dick Harcourt holds the bat. Standing left is Steve O'Brien (later to become Dr. O'Brien), sitting left is Ed O'Brien (later a lawyer), both sons of "Dad" O'Brien.

Peerless tobacco was the mainstay in all the camps. Strong enough to send a beginning user into a tailspin when he smoked his first pipeload, it was like meat and drink to the hard working men. They could work without whiskey during the winter months, but should they have been deprived of Peerless, they would have walked out of camp. They smoked it, they chewed it and sometimes used its ashes as snuff. Its smoke in the closed bunkhouses was suffocating to the uninitiated.

Traveling salesmen kept calling on Kilrane to sell him supplies for his camp, for his credit was excellent and he employed several hundred men. To supply his camp meant a good commission to the drummers, so they kept pestering the busy boss to buy. One tobacco salesman was particularly persistent and pressed Kilrane to buy his supply of Peerless. In exasperation Kilrane said:

"Sure, sure, send me a carload of Peerless."

A week later a railroad box car load of Peerless came in on the freight train, billed to Kilrane. Great wooden crates contained packages of the strong tobacco ranging from four ounces to ten pounds. Kilrane, good as his jesting words, accepted the enormous shipment, sold and gave away Peerless over a period of two years.

The rivalry which ran rampant between the crews of the various lumber camps found its equal in the intense jealousy and competition which existed between the youth of Seney and nearby towns. Trout Lake, Germfask, Newberry, Eckerman and other villages fought each other on the athletic fields, in the swimming and log rolling contests and in just fist and rock-throwing fights when they met.

Baseball games had their rabid fans. Gangs of rooters

accompanied the teams. An umpire or referee took his life in his own hands when he agreed to officiate a game or contest. Fights broke out on the sidelines. The winning team was often pelted with rocks or thrown into a nearby creek or river. Despite the intense rivalry and ill treatment received on the home grounds, the competition between the towns continued through the lusty days.

The kids and men and even some women had a name for anyone who lived in or around Seney. Anyone who claimed Seney as his home was a "Seney shit." Should any of them appear on the streets of a neighboring town they were immediately labeled and to this day that appelation can bring on a fight reminiscent of the 80ties.

CHAPTER TWENTY-TWO

The Battle of the Little Brown Jug

At Christmas time some of the married men spent their holiday with their families in Seney and nearby towns and farms. A few of the single men remained in camp and celebrated the season in their own fashion. Liquor was brought in in many devious ways in bottles and jugs, many of the men getting drunk and brawly.

Ed Cookson, as foreman, was a man who expected his crew to celebrate but he never allowed the men to get out of hand. He fed them well and hired the best cooks available, for food was the most important item to keep the men satisfied with their hard lot.

On the day before Christmas Cookson noticed that two of his men were well on their way to a drunken brawl. Doug Wilton, one of the supply teamsters, had made a visit to a nearby camp and had brought in a brown jug filled with whiskey. Tom Richards and Jim Haney had tipped the jug too often. Trouble was brewing as the pair began to show off their muscles and brag how they could take on any six men in camp.

Cookson decided to find the jug and put it out of commission. Knowing the ways of the drinkers, he searched the oat bin in the stables which was the usual hiding place of forbidden liquor. He found none there. He searched the mangers in the horse stable. Way down in the bottom of Wilton's team's stall he found the jug. Taking it outdoors he smashed it on the frozen ground, breaking it into small pieces and spilling the contents over the snow.

Wilton came around the corner of the stable and saw what had happened.

"Why did you break my little brown jug? I know your orders regarding liquor in camp. I don't give a damn about losing the whiskey. I know I had no right to bring it in. But to lose that poor little jug is just too much. It has been my friend for a long time. We've had so many good times together."

Cookson snorted:

"I meant what I said about bringing the stuff into camp. Now you'll have to suffer for it."

The foreman walked into the camp office while Wilton ran to the men's bunkhouse a few feet from the office to report his loss.

Within a few minutes Richards came out of the bunkhouse, storming, swearing and shouting what he would do to that So-and-So:

"I'll break his legs! I'll knock him into a cocked hat! I'll tear his head off."

Cookson heard the threats. He took up a hammer and placed it on the table where it would be handy in the event of trouble. He could hear the men trying to persuade Richards to forget the jug and calm down. Then he heard one of the crew say:

"Let him go. Cookson will take care of him."

The heavy stomp of Richard's boots sounded on the steps. Cookson opened the office door.

"What's on your mind, Richards? What can I do for

164

you?"

"Oh, nothing much," replied Richards meekly. "Wilton tells me you broke the little brown jug. I know that we had no right to go against the camp rule and bring in liquor and drink it in camp, but this is Christmas and we wanted to celebrate a little. But that brown jug! Wilton and I have drunk out of it so many times, it's like losing an old friend. I suppose I'll have to draw my time and leave camp."

"No," the camp boss told him. "If you fellows will straighten up and stop drinking in camp, I'll overlook it this time."

The next morning Richards came into the camp office and drew his time. Then taking his "turkey," he left for Seney. The taste of the liquor out of the little brown jug had been too much for him. Nothing would satisfy him now but to go where he could get a larger supply and stay until his stake was gone and he was ready to return to work. Cookson did not see him again that winter.

The next fall Richards appeared in camp again and applied for work. Cookson cautioned him:

"You know what my camp rules are and you know your failing. I don't want to be bothered by any jack who can't leave liquor alone while working for me. It makes the crew dissatisfied and it holds up the logging. I can't give you a job."

"I'll be honest with you, Ed. I want to go straight and work for you in your camp where I can get a good night's sleep after a hard day's work and good chuck. I'm tired of trying to sleep in a camp where there are a lot of drunken lumberjacks singing, fighting and making noise all night. I've made up my mind to cut out whiskey. I

165

can do it in your camp where it is not allowed."

Cookson, pitying the poor fellow, gave him another chance. Richards went to work and did not drink for the four months of the logging season. When the camp broke up he went with the others to Seney and indulged in one grand spree.

CHAPTER TWENTY-THREE

The Great Commoner Didn't Stop

WILLIAM JENNINGS BRYAN must have always remembered Seney. It was during his famous Gold and Silver campaign that his admirers tried to have his train stop at Seney for a few minutes on its way from Marquette to Saint Ignace but the local politicians were informed that due to a tight schedule it would be impossible.

Seney was a strongly Democratic community and the political bosses decided to take the matter into their own hands in typical Seney fashion as they had always done in the past. A careful scheme was laid to delay the train by ruse. Going down to the D.S.S.&A. railroad station, they secured an armful of railroad torpedoes which they placed on the rails all the way from the river bridge to the village. Two mammoth bonfires were prepared in the heart of town on both sides of the tracks. Barrels, wooden boxes and rubbish were saturated with kerosene, ready to be touched off at the sound of the train whistle.

It was planned that when the train stopped for water at the tank west of the Fox River, the men would light the fires so there would be a great blaze as the train pulled into town. Everything would have worked out successfully but someone had informed the conscientous Republican station agent, W. G. Miller, of the bold scheme.

Miller wired the Marquette station that there were

167

torpedoes on the tracks west of the village and asked the trainmen to ignore the explosions.

In the dark the whole population of Seney, well sprinkled with lumberjacks, awaited the whistle of the engine. It was midnight when the train roared in. The torpedoes went off with the sound of a sham battle. The train slowed down as its crew saw the bonfires lighting the skies but it kept going, with the silver-tongued Bryan sleeping peacefully in his berth. As the train reached the bonfires the negro porter stuck his head out of one of the windows. The crowd, thinking it was the Commoner, shouted:

"Hurrah for William Jennings Bryan!"

As the taillights of the last car faded into the distance, a lumberjack yelled above the disappointed crowd:

"To hell with William Jennings Bryan! Let's get a drink!"

General R. A. Alger, the head of the Alger-Smith Lumber Company, fared less well when he ran for governor of Michigan and appeared in Seney to solicit votes. His company, one of the biggest operators in the Upper Peninsula, was reaping a rich harvest by buying timber land cheaply and paying low wages in the camps and on the drive. His outfit continued the practise followed by many other concerns of cutting off "round forties"—buying a number of sections of timber land, then continuing to cut trees from adjacent areas owned by absentee people.

The Seney office of the company was notified of Alger's impending visit and ordered the foremen of the several Alger-Smith camps to stop logging and bring the whole force into Seney to greet their great employer and candidate. The town was packed with happy, roistering lum-

WILLIAM JENNINGS BRYAN FAILED TO STOP AT SENEY

Burton Historical Collections.

berjacks who began their celebration-with-pay early. They crowded the twenty or more saloons to overflowing and several minor fights were soon in progress. Dozens of barrels of beer were rolled into the vacant lots near the railroad station and the brew from Milwaukee flowed free and freely.

The gubernatorial train pulled in with whistle a-tooting and steam a-blowing. Men and women and children barged into the streets and surged toward the train. As the train stopped the General stood on the back platform and was introduced by one of the foremen as the friend of the lumberjack and the savior of the fair state of Michigan. Alger launched into his set speech and told the voters how he had started as a young man in the woods with nothing but his bare hands, and had by dint of hard work and saving risen to the high position he now occupied.

"My fellow workers, you, too, can do the same thing. Who knows but that some one of you will be governor of our great and glorious state?"

"You're a damned liar," shouted an inebriated blacksmith from one of the Alger-Smith camps. "You pay the lowest wages in this whole damned country."

That broke up the meeting and the blacksmith was rushed off to the Seney jail. Alger, embarassed by this sudden turn of events in his own bailiwick, stepped back into the coach and ordered the train to move on to the next town where a similar meeting had been arranged. The local justice of the peace fined the blacksmith $15.00 and thirty days in the village calaboose.

The foreman of the camp where the blacksmith was employed went to the Justice of the Peace, Murdock Morrison, and asked him to make it a cash fine so that the camp would not be deprived the services of its only black-smith. The fine was accordingly reduced to $15.00, which the company clerk promptly paid and hustled the in-surgent fellow back to camp to sober up in his straw bunk for his work the next day.

Alger stopped to visit the crew of men working on a log drive on the Fox River. He watched the operations for a time. Here he saw men working strenuously to keep the logs moving down the stream, at times waist deep in the icy water to free logs hung up on sand bars.

"How much are you paying these men?" asked Al-ger.

"We pay them plenty enough," replied the drive boss.

Not satisfied with this evasive answer, the General walked down to the river and asked one of the men what he was getting paid for that hard work.

"A dollar and seventy-five cents a day and chuck when we are near enough to the wanigan to eat."

Alger turned to the foreman and shouted:

"That's not enough for such work. Raise them."

The word of the raise in pay went up and down the river as if by wireless. The next morning the men were called together and informed that they would be paid the wages named by Alger up to date, but if they wanted to return to work it would be at the rate they had started with. The men threatened to walk off the job and strike out for Seney to get in touch by wire with Alger. How-ever, as they cooled off, they went back to the river one by one and finished the drive. General Alger became Gov-ernor Alger and the granddaddy of other politically in-spired Algers.

CHAPTER TWENTY-FOUR

You Can't Beat a Finn

ALTHOUGH the majority of the lumberjacks were American or Canadian born, many foreign-born men found their way to Seney and the camps in the Upper Peninsula. Among them were a few Finnish immigrants who found the weather conditions and the life in the pine country similar to that in their home land.

There were two types of Finnish immigrants who differed greatly in their habits, attitudes and skills. First was the Swedish Finn, who was a family man, religious, peaceful and a skilled worker. Docile and cooperative and ambitious to make a place in their new land, these men were readily accepted by the foremen in the camps. Sober, hard working and thrifty, they spent their winters in the woods to save enough money to buy a piece of land to clear and to build a log cabin to house their families the year around. At the end of the winter's work in the camps they went directly home to their families and began clearing their land, setting out crops and improving their holdings. They were good citizens seeking only the opportunity to improve their lot, raise and educate their children and find security in America.

The Russian Finns were of a different type. Accustomed to discrimination and rough treatment at the hands of their Russian overlords in their native land, they had developed over generations an attitude of hostility toward all authority. Those who escaped to America and to the pine land of Michigan were not as skilled as their Swedish cousins and were given only those jobs which required less responsibility. In the camps they worked as road monkies and other menial jobs. They were irascible and unfriendly except to their own.

Clannish to a degree, these Russian Finns drank heavily together and carried a short razor-sharp knife in their belts or boot tops for "social purposes." Woe to the man who crossed them or engaged them in a fight. Vicious, tenacious and unforgiving, they carried their grudges to extremes. Loyal to their own, they protected each other in trouble. They drank their clear grain alcohol straight.

A young tough from "down below" came into Dick Harcourt's saloon one spring when the men were down from the camps. He did not have the appearance of a woodsman and Harcourt eyed him suspiciously. When one of the Russian Finns came into the saloon and unrolled a handful of bills to pay for his drink of alcohol, the tough sided up to him and eyed the roll of greenbacks hungrily.

Harcourt leaned over the mahogany bar and whispered to the tough:

"You leave that Finlander alone or you'll get cut up."

Late that evening the young man was found in front of Scott's drug store covered with blood and staggering down the walk. John Bellaire asked him what had happened and was informed that he had been stabbed and was dying. Bellaire assisted him to Harcourt's saloon and ran for Dr. Bohn, the lone physician in town. The doctor removed the man's clothing and found that he

174

was covered with fifteen shallow knife slashes. It appeared that he had followed the Finn down the street and jumped him in a dark section. No money was found on the assailant, so it was concluded that his attack had been unsuccessful.

The next morning Jim Harcourt, the deputy sheriff, visited the home of Frank Aldo where the victim of the attack made his home. There was a large number of Finns present, sullen, incommunicative and brooding. To the deputy they all looked alike. He learned nothing from them. Mere hostile grunts were their only answers to his questions. The young tough spent two quiet weeks in a rooming house dressing his wounds, then took the train back to Bay City.

CHAPTER TWENTY-FIVE

They Ate the Evidence

T O THIS DAY the tale of how a shacker's wife outwitted the law and how the law ate the evidence is still going the rounds, with variations to fit the occasion.

Alex Lafere, a middle-aged lumberjack, lived up the Driggs River in a little log shack with his hard working wife. He worked some in the camps and on the drives but his pay check never reached home or the little woman. He always cashed it at Dunn's saloon to buy a few drinks for the boys, to pay off his debts for previous liquor and occasionally some of the "girls" at Dunn's "hoodlum" up the river "rolled" him for what he had left in his stagged pants.

In fits of rage Lefere would appear at home, beat his wife and kick out the windows of the shack. The life of the woman was one of fear, close to starvation at times and continual drudgery. When her husband was away from home she cut her own wood, banked the shack with snow to keep out the below zero winds and kept her lonely vigil. Neighbors supplied her with occasional food. Hunters left legs of venison in her woodshed to freeze and use as she needed meat.

One winter Lefere appeared at home in a drunken condition. Ed Cookson, the foreman at the Chicago Lumber Company camp, had fired him for bringing a jug of liquor into the camp. On his way to Seney he stopped at Dunn's hoodlum, cashed his time slip and made merry with the inmates. Then staggering home, he burst into the place and announced that he was leaving his wife for another woman and had come for his clothes.

"You might as well stay for dinner," his wife replied, thinking that a good meal and a few hours away from whiskey might bring him to his senses. "I cut some venison of that leg of deer in the shed and I baked a blueberry pie this morning. It's still hot in the oven."

"No, be jeez, I made up my mind," he yelled as he sat at the table counting the few pieces of change he had left from his pay.

He heard the door open and felt a blast of cold air as his wife went into the woodshed and returned. He started to turn to close the door when the little woman swung a leg of hard frozen venison over her head and crashed it over his skull. He slumped to the rough floor and lay still. She hung the leg of venison back on the hook in the shed.

With cold calculation, she swept out the shack, continued her cooking and sat down to eat her meal without looking at the corpse at her feet. She passed the night in undisturbed sleep.

The next morning dawned bright and crisp. Logging teams were passing on the road nearby, the runners squeeking loudly over the deep frozen snow. Taking a wooden snow shovel, she cleared a path from the door to the road and waited for the next load of logs to appear. A sturdy team of horses, their hides white with frost, came down the road. She hailed the driver:

"Something happened to my husband. Come in and

ROLLWAYS AT THE RAILROAD

Billions of Feet of Pine were drawn to the mills by rail.

Burton Historical Collections.

help me."

The teamster wound his reins to the binding chain and followed her. The sight of the dead man on the floor panicked the man and he ran out to the road to stop the other men as they drove up. Soon a dozen men trailed into the house, their heavy rubber-soled boots trampling down the snow. In their excitement and fear, they sought a clue to the killing. Their feet tracked back and forth, into the shed and out.

"I don't know how it happened," the woman explained. "I found him there last night when I came home from town in the snowstorm. When you get to the mill, please call the sheriff."

When the sheriff and his deputy appeared at noon, the woman was bowed down in grief and could give them no clue. The men examined the dead man, and pronounced his death due to a crushed skull. Systematically they searched the house and the grounds for the bludgeon with which the man was struck but found nothing. As they searched the woman began to prepare a meal. She brought the leg of venison from the shed and started to bake it in the oven of the wood stove.

Several hours passed. The Sheriff and his deputy remained puzzled. They went over every detail time and again. The early winter darkness had begun to settle down in the little shack as they prepared to leave, the mystery unsolved. The odor of roasting venison pervaded the air. The blueberry pie stood on the kitchen table and fresh baked bread came out of the oven.

"You men have been here a long time. You must be hungry. Better stay for supper. It is all ready," invited the tear-stained widow, wiping her hands on her apron.

The deputy looked at the sheriff and the sheriff nodded his head. Together the three ate at the rough, oilcloth covered table piled high with the fragrant food.

"This is wonderful venison, Mrs. Lafere," smiled the sheriff. "Wish my wife could cook a leg of venison like this. I like mine roasted with strips of bacon on top and a sprinkling of garlic."

The roast was half consumed before the hungry men pushed back from the table, their mouths blue from the pie.

The sheriff reached for his mackinaw and turned to the woman.

"We can't make head or tail how this happened to your man. We feel awfully sorry that you lost your husband. We'll take his body along with us in the sleigh and report that we couldn't find a clue. You know that a lot of men have been killed in this country and nobody ever found out how. This is just one of those cases. And thanks for the venison roast and the blueberry pie."

CHAPTER TWENTY-SIX

The Whitened Sepulchers of Seney

IN THE EARLY EIGHTIES a vast, almost endless forest of white pine extended from Ironwood on the west in the Upper Peninsula to Marquette on the north, to Saulte Ste. Marie on the east and to Escanaba on the south—giant trees which "would supply the entire country with lumber forever," so they said.

White pine stood thick, a few feet apart, some trees eight feet in diameter, with the first branches from sixty to eighty feet above the ground. The floor of the seemingly endless forest was clear of undergrowth, the trees so thick that no direct sunlight could reach the ground. In its virgin condition one could drive a team of horses and buggy between the trees anywhere except in the deep swamps. Pine needles and cones lay a foot or two thick on the floor, offering a soundless thoroughfare.

In the Seney area a million acres of land grew thick with trees which had started their way to the sky above when the pilgrims first landed on the forest-covered shores of New England. As the trees became aged their trunks decayed and fell under the blasts of the north winds which came down from stormy Lake Superior, to enrich the soil and feed new seedlings to take their places.

Few Indian trails crossed the primeval forest. Game was scarce, for the lack of undergrowth furnished no browse. It was only after the trees were felled and hauled to the river banks that hazel brush, pin cherries and spears of grass grew to feed deer, bear and rabbits. The streams teemed with speckled trout in their cold, crystal-clear waters. It was only after the great pine of southern Michigan became exhausted that the great lumber companies of that area moved across the Straits of Mackinaw to continue their onslaught on another "exhaustless" pine forest in the Seney swamp.

Came the Alger-Smith Lumber Company, the Chicago Lumber Company, the Bob Dollar Lumber Company and scores of others to Seney until fifteen lumber outfits were operating in the vicinity. Almost overnight from a collection of log buildings and crude lumber huts amid the mud and water, Seney became a self-supporting, roaring lumber town.

The advance guard were the timber lookers who scouted with tripod and record books the endless pine stands. Then the buyers for the exploiters came to buy the standing timber from settlers, the state land office and the railroad companies which had been granted free every alternate section of wooded land for extending their tracks into the wilderness. Thick stands of virgin pine was bought for between sixty-five cents and $1.25 per acre, which at today's market price would have brought $2625.00.

Next came the "wood butchers," the men who built the camps on the various holdings—built them of huge pine logs, covered them with tarpaper roofing, cut tiny holes for windows and chinked the cracks between the logs with moss and mud.

The camps completed, the lumberjacks came from the

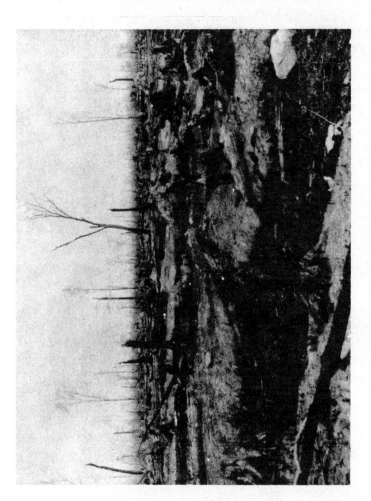

THE WHITENED SEPULCHERS OF SENEY

The end of the "endless" pine after the ravaging. A million acres of barren land, devastated and fruitless, surround the ghost town of Seney.

Timber Producers Association.

Saginaw Valley, the hill country of Cadillac, the plains of Grayling and the lumber regions of Quebec and New Brunswick. There came the Swedes from the pine country of Sweden, the Irish following the potato famine on the Old Sod, the Finns from the Arctic Circle, and a motley horde of camp followers, saloon keepers and gamblers.

Up the Fox River and the Driggs River and their tributaries went the men, teams of giant horses, sleighs, millions of feet of chain, axes, crosscut saws, cooks and camp bosses. A million acres of virgin pine lay before them. It was a job which challenged the operators as well as the "bulls-o'-the-woods." An early crew built dams on the rivers and creeks to hold back a "head" of water for the spring drives six months away, cleared the streams of obstructions which could cause a jam and built small log shacks along the waterways to house the river hogs as they came down with the "sticks" in the spring.

Seney, the little and unimportant, Seney, the little known settlement in the wilderness, became the hell hole of the north, more notorious for its size than the raw, rousing and insentimental town of Saginaw in its balmiest days. Seney, a crossroad settlement, was said to have been named for a Jewish fur buyer in its embryo days. Local residents have forgotten the origin of its name, but some declare it came from the fact that the fur buyer was known only as "sheeney" and the name was changed to its present form.

In its bawdiest days Seney boasted ten "hotels" with bars, and two mammoth bawdy houses on its outskirts as well as a score of smaller ones on its back streets. These "hoodlums," as they were called by the more respectable

THE WHITENED SEPULCHERS OF SENEY

citizens, became the dumping ground of the weaker elements and the holes into which was poured the hard-earned money of the men from the camps.

There were twenty-one saloons, two general stores, six drug stores, numerous meat markets, groceries and a jewelry store, the latter patronized chiefly by the "establishment" girls and loggers buying trinkets for them. The fifteen lumber companies and the several scores of camps poured their male population periodically into the town for drinking, fighting and "loving."

One tiny frame church took care of any religious inclination and there were seats available to all comers, too.

In this rugged, backwoods setting the onslaught on the "endless" pine began. Ruthless, grabbing for fortune, the lumber companies made most of the uncontrolled situation. With no thought for the lowly lumberjack and his welfare beyond using him as a beast of burden to hew out the standing timber, the operators did a complete job of it in fifteen short years. Slashing right and left, the prime pine was toppled to the ground, hauled to the skidways and rollways on the river banks, then ridden by the river hogs to the saw mills at Manistique or hauled to other mills in the north and south on logging trains whose tracks wound in and out of the vast forests.

The tops of fallen trees were left where they fell. Logs which had the slightest blemish remained on the ground to rot. A wierd tangle was left behind. As the crews moved to more profitable stands fires did the rest. The whitened sepulchers of Seney are the only witnesses of Michigan's pine today. Fires swept through the slashings unchecked, time and again, except when they threatened an operating camp. The intense heat of the resinous wood burned deeply into the ground consuming any humus which might be present. The burned over land had the appearance of a modern battlefield where army after army had fought back and forth over the same territory.

Today for fifty or more miles around Seney and the former scene of endless white pine stand millions of whitened sepulchers in the shape of pine stumps, thick, white and high, now a cemetery like the bleached markers which dot the fields of Flanders. Mile upon mile of stumps, forlorn reminders of what once was, meet the eye as one drives over the sand trails about the formerly notorious town. These whitened stumps rise from four to ten feet above the ground, indicating the depth of the snow when the trees were felled. A few pin cherry trees with their bitter fruit and a few stunted blueberry bushes still raise their heads, striving vainly to offer their once sweet berries in a soil which no longer holds sustenance.

Said an oldtimer:

"The land is so poor that a crow has to carry his own lunch across it."

The creeks and rivers, once flooded each spring to carry millions of straight-grained pine logs to the mills below, now rise feebly each spring in an urge to reach their mother of waters, Lake Michigan, then soon shrink in feeble volume. The soil which had previously jealously retained the precious water under the vast roof of protecting pine and deep root systems, no longer holds the rains and snow water but is in turn washed into the streams, thus robbing the land of whatever nourishment it might have had.

188

Gone long since are the lumber barons with the fortunes they gleaned by ruthless methods and cheap labor, gone to the great cities, Chicago, Detroit, Boston and New York, where they invested their gains in railroad-stock, the auto industry and other fast moving ventures. Behind them they left abandoned lumber camps, the stranded lumberjacks and their families, the ghost towns which supplied them with labor and the centers of operations.

Of the timber barons it was said:

"They were a thieving crew addicted to muttonchop whiskers and piling up vast sums of money. Time, however, had given them the status of empire builders, and their larceny is remembered only by a few diligent historians (like this author), who do not count."

Across the mound of years their rapacity has placed upon the following generation a burden which will be hard to bear but always remembered.

Seney, once a prosperous, thriving, bustling town of 3000, which was swelled to double that number when the camps broke up in the spring, now counts carefully its 250 souls, 32 dwellings, 4 gas stations, a bar, two general stores, a small factory living on the forest gleanings, a small community house, a grade school and a few modern homes. The town is almost completely surrounded by the creeping in of jackpine and scrubs which now cover much of the town whose once proud buildings have either burned to the ground or were torn down or removed.

"Boot Hill," the burying ground where many nameless and forgotten people were interred, sits on a small rise of ground at the edge of the village, overgrown with jackpine and brush, with graves neglected and sunken. Old obliterated grave markers have toppled over, totally

189

neglected. The once decorative iron fence has rusted down. A deer trail crosses the graves as the animals travel from swamp to swamp. "Boot Hill" remains neglected by the township officials and no voice rises in protest in memory of the souls whose bodies were laid at rest in the little plot.

Jack Mitchell, a former lumber camp foreman and river boss, lives in a modest home with his wife, a few rods from Boot Hill. Jack wanted to accompany the author to the cemetery. Together they entered the sagging gate and walked over foot-deep pine needles and broken branches to examine the final resting place of many oldtimers. As they passed from grave to grave and looked down into the sunken ground, tears came to the old man's eyes and overflowed his wrinkled cheeks. Wiping his once rugged face with a hand which had rolled many a log at the skidway, he remarked:

"I hope that when my turn comes my last resting place will not be so neglected."